378·
154
We
HE

KU-319-216

Researching Foundation Degrees

LINKING RESEARCH AND PRACTICE

Edited by Peter Beaney

fdf Publications
London and Lichfield

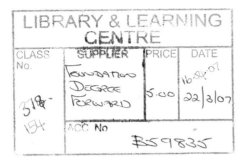

LIBRARY & LEARNING CENTRE

CLASS No.	SUPPLIER	PRICE	DATE
318· 134	Foundation Degree Forward	5.00	16·04·07 22/3/07
	ACC No BS9835		

Published by Foundation Degree Forward *(fdf)*

Copyright © The Editor and Contributors, 2006

All rights reserved. No reproduction, copy or transmission of this publication may be made without the written permission of the publishers, save in accordance with the provisions of the Copyright, Designs and Patents Act 1988, or under the terms of any licence permitting limited copying issued by the Copyright Licensing Agency.

www.fdf.ac.uk

ISBN 1-905917-00-7

An olive design 01785 272931. Printed in Great Britain by GoodmanBaylis, Worcester

Contents

Page

Acknowledgements   v

Notes on Contributors   vi

List of Acronyms   ix

Editor's Introduction   1

Peter Beaney, Foundation Degree Forward

Part 1: The Research Context   7

1.   Research, Policy, And Practice: the case of Foundation degrees   8

Peter Beaney, Foundation Degree Forward

2.   Rethinking Research and Development   32

Andrew Morris, National Educational Research Forum

Part 2: Quantitative and Qualitative Approaches   45

3.   Provision and Participation: using quantitative research to explore foundation degree provision.   46

Amanda Nelson, Quality Assurance Agency

4.   Recovering the Student Voice: retention and achievement on Foundation degrees   74

Daphne Hampton and Margo Blythman, London College of Communication, University of the Arts London

Contents

Part 3: Aspects of Practice – Assessment, Curriculum   **95**
        Development and Work-Based Learning

5.   Foundation Degree Assessment Models: meeting the needs   **96**
      of the new generation of higher level students on hospitality
      management Foundation degrees
      Conor Sheehan, Westminster Kingsway College

6.   Foundation Degrees and Partnership Approaches to Curriculum   **123**
      Development and Delivery
      Mike Doyle, University of Salford

7.   Work Based Learning and Foundation Degrees: exploring   **146**
      assessment as an active process of student choice and engagement
      Laurence Solkin, City University London

Part 4: Appendices   **161**

Appendix 1:   **162**
Bibliography of Research and Scholarship Regarding
Foundation Degrees

Appendix 2:   **172**
Researching Foundation Degrees: contacts and resources
to support research

Acknowledgements

The editor would like to thank the following:

All of the contributors to this volume who have worked hard to ensure its completion.

Foundation Degree Forward *(fdf)* for funding and supporting the development of this edited publication.

Janet Wyatt *(fdf)*, Nina Johnson (Olive Design) and Karen Hibbert (proof reader) for their work on the production of this publication.

Bryan Brown for his support with the research agenda around Foundation degrees.

Derek Longhurst and my colleagues at *fdf* who helped when times were hard!

My family (Cherry, Laura, Emily and Victoria) for making it all worthwhile.

Peter Beaney, 5th July 2006

Notes on contributors

Peter Beaney (editor) is Research Fellow with Foundation Degree Forward *(fdf)* where he has been involved in supporting, developing and carrying out research with respect to Foundation degrees and related areas of learning and teaching. His current research and writing focuses upon the development of an agenda at national level for Foundation degree research and scholarship and the role which work-based learning plays in the design, development and delivery of Foundation degrees. With respect to Foundation degree research, the subject of this volume, he is concerned primarily with the relationship between research, policy and practice and how this set of relationships can be both understood and changed. This carries forward into his research on work-based learning which seeks to set this within the wider context of major changes in the relationship between learning and work. In the past he has carried out research in Latin America (on social movements and rural development) and in Scotland (on the Scottish electronics industry). His main interests in terms of learning and teaching practice are in the development of community, work-based and virtual learning in a range of settings and with a wide range of different learners.

Margo Blythman is Director of Teaching and Learning at the London College of Communication, University of the Arts London. Her responsibilities include staff development, the quality of teaching and learning, tutorial systems and study support. She has published on such topics as retention, development strategies within higher education contexts and the development of student academic writing, particularly in the context of Art and Design. Her academic interests also include the impact of quality assurance systems on the working lives of academic staff and micropolitics in UK higher education.

Mike Doyle is Head of Access Development and Widening Participation in the Education Development Unit at the University of Salford. As an education developer his main emphasis has been on curriculum innovation to reach new learners in new sites of learning. Work-based learning and Foundation degrees have, therefore, been core aspects of his professional development and research activity. He is currently undertaking research and writing up a PhD at Lancaster University which focuses on collaborative approaches to curriculum development within Foundation degrees. He has published the results of his research and development work in a range of journals and international conference proceedings.

Daphne Hampton is an academic member of staff at the London College of Communication, University of the Arts London. She is the Student Mentor Co-ordinator for the College, a member of the study support team, and Tutorial Co-ordinator for one of the schools in the College. She combines research into student mentoring with the practical experience of running student mentoring schemes over several years and has acted as a consultant in this field. Her research and publication interests are the first year student experience on Foundation degrees, student mentoring and personal academic tutoring.

Andrew Morris was until recently the Director of NERF (National Educational Research Forum), a body established by the government to provide a forum for discussing the relevance and appropriateness of educational research. NERF has recently taken on charitable status but continues to work on issues in relation to 'D&R' ('Development and Research') in relation to education in all of its forms. Andrew has published and presented widely on these issues and has been a notable contributor to debates concerning the relevance of research, practitioner research, and evidence-based practice.

Amanda Nelson is the Head of the Information Unit at the QAA (Quality Assurance Agency for Higher Education), leading on information, research and analysis pertaining to higher education within the UK. She has particular responsibility for the monitoring and evaluation of TQI (Teaching Quality Information). In addition, Amanda remains an Honorary Research Associate of the University of Worcester, where she was previously employed as a Lecturer in Geography specialising in spatial criminology and research methods. Amanda has also worked as the Head of Analytical Services for a

UK police force. She is an Independent Member of the Gloucestershire Police Authority and Fellow of the Royal Geographical Society. Current research activities include student spatial behaviour; student engagement in higher education and young people's fear of crime.

Conor Sheehan is Programme Leader for Hospitality, Leisure and Tourism at Westminster Kingsway College. The College is a General Further Education College in Central London with over 20,000 students on eight sites. Conor is currently also working during part of his time carrying out research work for the Sussex Lifelong Learning Network and the School of Service Management at the University of Brighton. He has published and given papers on Foundation degrees in the hospitality area with funding from, amongst others, the Higher Education Academy Subject Centre for Hospitality, Leisure, Sport and Tourism.

Laurence Solkin is Programme Director for Work-Based Learning at City University and is responsible for a range of programmes in professional development. These programmes are intended to develop and support communities of professional practice through the use of formal teaching, action learning and supported e-learning. Laurence was previously a manager of learning in public sector organizations, focusing on staff development and is a Chartered Member of the Charter Institute of Personnel and Development. More recently he has been an academic specializing in organizational change and self development at Birkbeck College, London Guildhall University and currently at City University. His doctoral research explored the impact of assessment on work-based learning. Current research activities mainly revolve around work-based learning for public service professionals within Foundation degree programmes. Laurence is also a member of the National Advisory Committee to the public services section of the GMB trade union and is undertaking research on the identity of trade unions members in the public sector.

List of acronyms

APEL	Accreditation of Prior and Experiential Learning
ASN	Additional student numbers
BA	Bachelor of Arts
CAA	Computer aided assessment (CAA)
CMC	Computer mediated communication
D&R	Development and research
DfES	Department for Education and Skills
EPPI-	Evidence for Policy and Practice Information and Co-ordinating Centre
ESRC	Economic and Social Research Council
eTMA	Electronic tutor marked assignment
fdf	Foundation Degree Forward
FE	Further education
FEC	Further education college
FHEQ	Framework for Higher Education Qualifications
FTE	Full-time equivalent
HE	Higher education
HE in FE	Higher education (delivered) in further education
HEFCE	Higher Education Funding Agency for England
HEI	Higher education institution
HESA	Higher Education Statistical Agency
HNC	Higher National Certificate
HND	Higher National Diploma

ILT	Institute of Learning and Teaching
JACS	Joint Academic Coding System
LCC	London College of Communication
	(a constituent college of the University of the Arts London)
LSDA	Learning and Skills Development Agency
LSN	Learning and Skills Network
MA	Master of Arts
NERF	National Educational Research Forum
NQF	National Qualifications Framework
NVQ	National Vocational Qualification
OECD	Organisation for Economic Cooperation and Development
PCET	Post Compulsory Education and Training
PDP	Personal development planning
QAA	Quality Assurance Agency
R&D	Research and development
RDA	Regional Development Agency
SSC	Sector Skills Council
TLRP	Teaching and Learning Research Programme
UCAS	Universities & Colleges Admissions Service
VLE	Virtual learning environment

Editor's Introduction

Themes

This book has a number of central and inter-related themes. The main, and connecting, theme is to do with the role of research in relation to policy and practice with respect to Foundation degrees. The latter, however, don't exist in isolation; they are part of a wider set of relationships and, because of their innovatory features, exemplify some of the key aspects of contemporary changes in learning provision.

Foundation degree research

Foundation degrees are, nevertheless, relatively under-researched and this theme is explored in some detail in the first part of the book in terms of a detailed and contextualising look at the current state and future development of Foundation degree research (Chapter 1). Part 1 also contains a broader examination, by Andrew Morris, of the relationship between research and development which he characterises, in a provocative inversion of terms, as 'development and research' (D&R). In a sense the substantive contributions to this collection both illustrate and contradict this general theme in that they are all by 'practitioners' of one kind or another, who have been working in different ways and in different parts of the educational system to develop, support or deliver Foundation degrees. Research has thereby become part of their normal activity in terms, for example, of their own professional development or broader involvement with evaluating and enhancing the quality of learning and teaching. None of them, I suspect, would characterise themselves as professional 'researchers', although research might make up a large and potentially growing part of their remit. They are exceptional,

---

Note: The opinions expressed in this book are those of the editor and authors and not necessarily those of Foundation Degree Forward.

however, in that they are publishing and disseminating this work through a variety of media and events in a way which isn't yet characteristic of the field as a whole.[1]

Research and practice

The second main theme has to do with the relationship between research and practice. 'Practice' is a central concept in relation to Foundation degrees in a variety of ways. It points, for example, to differences in the learning which characterise in 'vocational' (practical, applied) and 'academic' (theoretical, conceptual) learning. This is the sense, for example, in which 'theory' is frequently opposed to 'practice'. The latter is also a central category in professional education and training for the 'old' professions – health, medicine, law - where proficiency in professional 'practice' is frequently an essential, if contested, category. It is used more specifically in particular occupational settings – in, for example, performance and the creative industries - to refer to the centrality of being able to perform in particular ways to specific standards as a result of consistent and systematic 'practice'.

Foundation degrees, as is now well known, are orientated towards occupations which are widely characterised as belonging to the 'associate professional' and 'advanced technician' occupational groups but as professional boundaries are becoming more permeable and labour processes more differentiated, the divisions between different groups may shift over time. As Mike Doyle observes in his chapter (Ch. 6) in Part 3, there was very little difference between the processes affecting his students, working within the public sector, and those affecting staff delivering a Foundation degree at a university undergoing restructuring and job redesign. We can only understand these processes and their relationship to, for example, the experience of work based learning through research. Mike Doyle also reveals the complexities of partnership arrangements between HE, FE and employers which are affected by different preconceptions and practices in relation to the learning process which have to be worked through if they are not to be a stumbling block to development. Similarly, Conor Sheehan in his contribution (Ch. 5) analyses the responses of providers, employers and learners in terms of their involvement in different types of assessment and, in particular, the use of online assessment to provide flexibility and access.

The student experience

The third main theme is one that is probably the most under-represented at the moment and that is the student experience. Given the centrality of innovative forms of learning (work based, flexible, blended and reflective learning) to Foundation degrees it is confounding to find that the learner's experience of engaging with the new qualification is so under examined. If Foundation degrees are to be successful and genuinely transformative in terms of both economic modernisation and social inclusion, we need to understand how students respond to them and how they can best utilise their learning experience over time to engage in 'lifelong learning'. In particular, we need to understand the differences between full-time learners (part-time workers) and full-time workers (part-time learners) in terms of their learning experiences. Are there differences in quantity and quality which distinguish between these two ideal typical categories of learners? Is one to be preferred to the other in terms of quality of outcomes? Is this a viable distinction given the well known engagement of full-time students in various forms of part-time work? How can we best support Foundation degree students and ensure that they engage with and are retained within their learning programme? The latter issues are addressed here in the chapter by Daphne Hampton and Margo Blythman (Ch. 4) which focuses on the 'student voice' and the need to examine what this can tell us regarding the achievement and retention of students on to Foundation degree programmes. Their extensive use of student testimony reveals that the student experience is quite diverse, although there are similarities of experience which can usefully point towards ways of modifying institutional processes in relation to student support, the timing of contact sessions, and the ways in which we regard, value and refer to 'non-traditional' learners.

'Doing research'

The fourth theme relates more to how we research Foundation degrees rather than to what we research. Part 2 of the book presents two contrasting pieces of research: that by Daphne Hampton and Margo Blythman (Ch. 4) referred to above, which is primarily qualitative and small scale, and the work of Amanda Nelson at QAA (Ch. 3) who provides one of the first reliable quantitative overviews of the characteristics of Foundation degree students, using data which QAA gathered during its 2005 review of the qualification. These two different approaches are both valuable but tell us very different things about Foundation degree learners, their experiences, origins and social and educational backgrounds. We do, however, need both and I would argue that there are no grounds for prioritising one over the other in terms of producing 'evidence' based practice even though in policy circles 'hard data' is currently valorised over 'softer' forms of research. It is very difficult, for example, to interpret and understand the data which Amanda Nelson presents without some qualitative information to underpin this and help us to determine what the data may be pointing to. Similarly the qualitative analysis needs to be augmented by more quantitative data if we want to know how generalised or not these experiences are. More specifically perhaps, we need to engage with the difficulties and opportunities that these different forms of research present as well as the professional development which researchers, practitioners and other professionals require to not only carry out but also to negotiate and interpret research findings. One of the implications of Andrew Morris' chapter (Ch. 2) is that we need to look at the research process as something which is much more than just 'doing research'. If we want research 'to count' we need to look at who is commissioning, who is funding and who is benefiting from research as well as who is doing it. We might also want, as is suggested in my chapter (Ch. 1), to think about different ways of 'doing research' which build upon the strengths of Foundation degrees in terms of building partnerships and enlisting employer involvement to deliver more collaborative and workplace based research. At the same time, research should not be an isolated or elite activity; it overlaps with other activities – e.g. enquiry based learning, the scholarship of learning and teaching, evaluation and monitoring, and the professional development of teachers and learning support staff - in ways which potentially extend the value and democratise the use of research.

Work and work based learning

The last main theme relates to the relationship between Foundation degrees and different forms of work, occupation, profession and employment. Part 3 looks at different aspects of 'practice' in terms of assessment, collaborative curriculum design and work based learning. Laurence Solkin's chapter (Ch. 7) addresses some of these issues when he looks at work based learning in relation to learner assessment. He explores the tensions and possibilities which lie between academic assessment of learners and work based assessment or appraisal of employees. Although there is a large and developing literature on work based learning in HE there is very little on work based learning in relation to the acquisition of the intermediate level knowledge and skills represented by Foundation degrees. Indeed, some would question the use of analytical categories such as 'skill' in contexts where they haven't traditionally been used before (e.g. 'employability skills'). Foundation degrees are, however, indelibly linked to the wider economic policy agenda around developing the intermediate level workforce skills which are seen to characterise associate professional and advanced technician categories of employment. A series of government skills reports have highlighted this as a critical area for development in relation to England's comparator nations in Europe, North America and East Asia. For decades this has been a consistent theme of both economic and educational policy-making in terms of the lack of a high quality vocational option that would rival the long established 'academic' route. Whereas Europe, and increasingly Wales and Scotland, seek to provide vocational and academic 'tracks' which are equally valued and closely linked in terms of potential 'cross over', England has thus far failed to develop this. In this respect there is a dearth of research about how Foundation degrees link into other systems and networks – from information, advice and guidance systems to learning partnerships and vocationally based progression routes – which contribute both to facilitating the quality of learning and learner employability and the effectiveness of the vocational learning system in meeting the needs of the economy. Such issues are experienced differently in different employment sectors as the different contributions here on the Hospitality industry (Conor Sheehan), Public Services (Mike Doyle, Laurence Solkin) and Art and Design (Daphne Hampton and Margo Blythman) demonstrate. Within particular professions and occupations there are learning cultures and practices which shape how learners, and particularly 'novice' learners, learn as well as how they are introduced into a particular practitioner community. The prevalence of problem based learning (PBL) in health is one well known example but there are others, which are perhaps less well known. These relationships are as yet little understood in terms of particular subjects and sectors, as are the current transformations in work processes and new categories of professional (e.g. teaching assistants), yet they may be central to the learner experience of work based learning.

An agenda for Foundation degree research?

In sum, then, there are a wealth of opportunities which are open to Foundation degree research and scholarship, some of which are explored here in this collection of analysis and case studies. However without a concerted and systematic effort to support this research the initial experience of designing, developing and delivering Foundation degrees will be lost. There is a lack of both in-depth qualitative and quantitative research which is due to a range of factors from intellectual snobbery and resistance to the 'new vocationalism', on the one hand, to the limited investment by research and funding organisations in what have hitherto been marginalised spheres of learning, on the other. Practitioner research alone cannot compensate for this lack as it is frequently done under difficult and resource poor circumstances. Rather there needs to be a longer term and strategic investment in achieving this goal if we are to see new forms of education which empower rather than disadvantage vocational learners.

Notes

[1] For a detailed bibliography of research based work which has been published on Foundation degrees see Appendix 1 of this volume.

1

The Research
Context

Chapter 1

Research, Policy and Practice

THE CASE OF FOUNDATION DEGREES

Peter Beaney
Foundation Degree Forward[1]

Introduction

Since the government first announced the introduction of Foundation degrees in February 2000 a great deal has been done to try to establish them as a successful and sustainable form of higher education. As a new and potentially radical form of employment-focused learning, Foundation degrees have been underpinned by substantial funding and an emergent institutional infrastructure which has been designed to ensure that not only are they sustainable but they meet the different needs of the economy, employers and learners. It is not clear, however, that there has been a corresponding effort in terms of supporting the development of Foundation degrees through the growth of an appropriate body of research and scholarship (Beaney 2005a and 2005b). Currently we know very little about how Foundation degrees are developing and it is therefore difficult to make informed judgements about critical issues such as their success in meeting their intended outcomes, the social constituencies which they recruit, and the dynamics of their production (e.g. employer engagement, educational partnerships and professional recognition). From a more instrumental point of view, the relative absence of research and scholarship around Foundation degrees undermines the process of evaluation and revision which policy-makers, educational institutions and practitioners need to undertake if the new qualification is to survive in the face of rapidly changing economic conditions. Unfortunately, this situation doesn't seem to be improving very much over time as there have been few signs of growth in research activity over the last few years[2]. Although formal academic research activity isn't the only indicator, the fact that there have been only a handful of scholarly articles published on Foundation degrees since their inception, and no monographs, is at least one significant indicator of the limited level of research activity.[3][4] This chapter is, therefore, an attempt to draw attention to this situation, to map out what has been done in terms of investigating Foundation degrees, and to explore what might be done to construct a research agenda for the future. Such a project also inevitably raises fundamental issues about the purpose, effectiveness and appropriateness of educational research in an applied setting, and these issues are addressed in this paper where they throw light on the particular questions being addressed. The emphasis, however, is on how the particular case raises questions about general principles and approaches; not how general debates illuminate the case.

It would be wrong, given what has been said above, to underestimate what has been done to understand Foundation degrees to date, even if this has not been done within the context of formal academic research. There are things which we do know as a result, for example, of successive QAA (Quality Assurance Agency) reviews (see QAA 2003 and 2005b), publicly funded evaluation studies, and practitioner-based research. In some respects the contents of this volume are also a testament to the work of those who have engaged with this area because of their diverse relationships to it in practice. Practitioners working in universities, colleges, and intermediary and supporting institutions have been concerned to ensure that Foundation degree development does not go ahead unmarked and unrecorded. Given its small scale and under-funded nature, however, this activity can only provide a very partial and fragmentary view.

It might be argued that it is too early to expect much research but Foundation degrees have been under discussion and development for some time – since at least the late 1990s - and they have not as yet attracted anything like the attention received by, for example, national vocational qualifications (NVQs) at the time that they were launched. In this chapter I am not necessarily concerned so much with why this is the case but rather with the more practical question of what we already know and how we know it as well as what we would like to know if the research base could be built. These are relatively naïve questions in theoretical terms but they reflect both the limited state of development of Foundation degree research and the instrumental aim of wanting to develop an agenda for Foundation degree research[5]. It is also worth noting at this point that I am endeavouring to make few assumptions about what properly constitutes educational 'research' or, by implication, who should conduct it, where it should be located and what it should focus upon. Rather I am taking the view that there are different ways of 'doing' educational research (e.g. formal academic, action- and practitioner-based research) as well as different ways of utilising or engaging with it. I am also assuming that these different approaches have their different strengths and one is not necessarily superior to the other in any way. This is important since I also want to consider, to the extent that it is possible here, ways in which educational research might be defined in unconventional ways in order to facilitate a closer relationship with policy and practice.

As is well known, educational research has been severely criticised on a number of grounds since the late 1990s but my purpose isn't to review these critiques again (see Silver 1999 and Hammersley 2002 for overviews from different perspectives) but rather to ask the question, from the point of view of someone closely involved in supporting Foundation degree development: how can research best serve policy and practice in terms of enhancing the quality of Foundation degrees for learners, employers and educational institutions? This necessarily impinges on the ongoing educational research debate but also raises different issues given, in particular, the fact that Foundation degrees, almost uniquely, involve the representation and accommodation of different social interests by virtue of the fact that they are developed, designed and delivered collaboratively.

What do we already know about Foundation degrees?

The main thing that makes Foundation degrees of wider interest than simply a new form of employment focused provision is that they are potentially groundbreaking in terms of their conception and delivery. They are also an ongoing experiment in educational re-engineering since they are implicated in a wide range of government policy agendas; including, for example, raising workforce skills, reforming vocational education and widening access to higher education. It is this that makes them an exemplary case for research and a test case for many of the transformations taking place in educational policy and practice - in all sectors of education - at the current time. As the Foundation Degree Task Force Report (2004) notes:

> "The Foundation degree is a bold innovation, incorporating many dimensions – any one on its own would be challenging, and taken together they have the potential to stimulate a radical reorientation of higher education provision. The White Paper set the Foundation degree the challenge of 'breaking the traditional pattern of demand'. In practice, that also means breaking strongly-embedded patterns of supply. It means succeeding where previous attempts have failed in raising the status of vocationally-oriented courses and the credibility of 'two year' higher education qualifications." *(DfES, 2004: p. 5)* [6]

Foundation degrees are, then, at the heart of a complex set of changes in educational 'supply and demand' which are closely linked at an institutional level to reforms of educational provision through, for example, the redefinition of 14-19 education, changes in the NQF (National Qualifications Framework) and attempts to bridge the academic/vocational 'divide'. At a more general level, these reforms link to structural changes in the nature of work, employment and lifelong learning which bear directly upon our inherited assumptions about the purpose(s) of education. The debate concerning the latter has elicited highly polarised positions as to, for example, the role of education in preparation for work, meeting employer needs, and developing employability and enterprise. Providing direct entry into specific vocations has generally been rejected within the liberal tradition and the 'new vocationalism' has therefore been highly contested within universities and other providers of HE (for a sense of the debate see: Avis et al 1996; Avis 2003; Lea et al 2003; Young 1993; and Young and Spours 1997).

As is the case, however, with any major change it is difficult to grasp the nature, scale and pace of the change whilst it is taking place. In many respects this is one of the principal roles which, in a naïve way, we might expect research to play: to tell us about 'what is going on', to establish what is successful and what is not, and to piece together from the 'evidence' an overview to inform future policy and practice. However, as recent responses to critiques of educational research have unfailingly pointed out, there are complex issues which intervene when we try to obtain such a simple picture of 'reality'. What criteria do we use, for example, to judge what is successful or not? Who decides what is 'useful knowledge' in terms of improving practice in the work place and the academy? How do we identify the priority areas in which to concentrate scarce resources? Whilst researchers may debate or defer such decisions practitioners have to address, on a daily basis, the question 'what is to be done?' Recognising, therefore, that any attempt to characterise a complex social reality is partial and value-laden but also recognising that there are moral as well as political imperatives involved in attempting to bridge the gap between research and practice I want to try to undertake the task of characterising the current state of our understanding of Foundation degrees, the context in which they operate and the investigations which have brought us to this understanding.

Foundation degrees have their roots in the policy debates of the 1990s concerning economic decline, the 'skills gap' between the UK and its competitors, the inadequacies of the existing vocational and training system, and the need for a response to these issues from within compulsory and post-compulsory education. A series of reports in the 1990s looked at the possibility of linking 'short cycle' intermediate qualifications with a vocational emphasis to the shortage of skilled workers at associate professional and higher technician level and the need to facilitate access to higher education via the creation of a vocational or work-based route. At the same time, two year 'associate degrees' along the lines of the US 'Community College' model were widely seen as a solution to the need to both expand access to higher education and 'upskill' the workforce. The government's extensive review of workforce skills in a series of National Skills Task Force reports from the late 1990s onwards suggested a deficit in precisely those employment sectors which the short-cycle and vocationally orientated associate degrees were meant to address: i.e. those forms of employment, such as the newly emerging associate professionals in health and education (e.g. teaching assistants), which required skills somewhere between routine and professional skills. Not surprisingly these were also employment sectors undergoing major redefinitions in terms of the division of labour between different categories of staff and pressures for the recognition of their professional or associate professional status.

The latter were identified early on by government as an area in which major employment growth was likely to take place and where, consequently, there was a need for a response from within education. As is clearly demonstrated in the earliest Foundation degree policy documents, the best known intermediate level higher education qualifications with an employment focus, HNCs (Higher National Certificates) and HNDs (Higher National Diplomas), had peaked in terms of recruitment in the 1990s and were in relative decline. They were also part of a labyrinthine system of vocational qualifications which was confusing for both employers and learners as well as limited in terms of progression into higher education (DfEE 2000: 25-27). More worryingly perhaps, vocational qualifications in England have, in comparison to their continental counterparts, never achieved anything approaching parity with the more prestigious academic route into higher education which has been a predominantly middle class preserve (and still is to a large extent). By contrast vocational education has been either invisible in both research and policy terms or seen as confined to the further education sector - itself widely characterised as a 'Cinderella service' vis-à-vis secondary and higher education[7]. This situation has changed substantially in recent times as a result not only of new policies to redefine further education within a wider 'learning and skills' or PCET (Post-Compulsory Education and Training) sector but also the increasing recognition of the role of further education in higher education and in Foundation degrees in particular8.

Given the complexity of the policy 'drivers' outlined above it is not surprising that the new qualification was established with a complex set of 'core characteristics'. The QAA Foundation degree qualification benchmark (2004) identifies these as follows:

> "The distinctiveness of Foundation degrees depends upon the integration of the following characteristics: employer involvement; accessibility; articulation and progression; flexibility; and partnership. While none of these attributes is unique to Foundation degrees, their clear and planned integration within a single award, underpinned by work-based learning, makes the award very distinctive." (QAA 2004: p. 5)

Figure 1: Stages in the Development of Foundation degrees
The relatively short period of existence of Foundation degrees can be divided into a number of key stages:

Gestation
The evolution during the 1990s of the idea, as noted above, that the development of a new form of short-cycle higher education was required as a response to the skills gap at intermediate level and to widen access to higher education.

Pilot Phase
From February 2000 the government launched its Foundation degree initiative through first a general consultation (DfEE 2000) and secondly the publication of a prospectus inviting the development of prototype Foundation degrees by consortia of further and higher education providers linked with employers. In the first phase HEFCE (Higher Education Funding Council for England) supported a limited number of prototypes which

were seen as a learning experiment to lay the basis for the more general adoption of the qualification within the further and higher education sectors. The prototypes were relatively well funded but heavily scrutinised and had to undergo very rapid development in order to meet HEFCE's target of delivery in autumn 2001.

Roll Out

From 2002 all institutions were able to bid for ASNs (additional student numbers) to support the delivery of Foundation degrees and there was a quite rapid expansion in the number of funded Foundation degree places.

Expansion

In recent years there have been successive generations of Foundation degrees which have been accompanied by expansion in both student numbers and the number and range of Foundation degrees on offer. Expansion has also been accompanied by very close scrutiny in quality assurance terms as the sector has undergone two QAA reviews in relatively short succession.

As Figure 1 illustrates, the brief history of Foundation degree development can be separated into a number of phases. There is a substantial amount of consistency in policy concerns over this period but also shifts and changes in emphasis between the different components of the overall strategy. During the most recent phases of development Foundation degrees have undergone marked expansion in terms of student numbers, the range of vocational areas, and the number of educational providers involved. In the initial phases of setting up and recruitment much of the provision was focused on the public sector – education, health, public administration, policing – but there are signs of greater diversification. Foundation degrees have also undergone two major rounds of quality assessment by QAA which reflects the government's concern to ensure the quality of provision and that the new award is protected against allegations of 'dumbing down'. The student profile has been difficult to establish with any certainty given the statistical difficulties of cross-institutional provision but there is much greater involvement of mature students and full-time modes of attendance than perhaps originally expected for an award that has sometimes been identified as focusing on 'those already in work'. The social constituencies on which Foundation degrees draw are in fact much more complex than this would suggest and subject to change, as the preponderance of female students – probably linked to the preponderance of public over private sector – in the first generations of Foundation degrees would seem to suggest.

At the time of writing, the Foundation degree can be characterised as a new vocationally focused qualification which forms part of an emerging framework of more work-based learning pathways. In contrast to HNC/HNDs, however, Foundation degrees place much greater emphasis upon the achievement of high level academic learning outcomes and, in particular, the integration of academic and work-based learning. They are particularly distinctive perhaps in being the result of structured partnerships between higher education and further education providers and employers with the latter expected to be closely involved in the design, development and delivery of the qualification. At the same time, Foundation degrees are closely articulated with an emerging framework of employer (Sector Skills Councils), professional and economic development organisations (Regional Development Agencies) which the government expects to be at the forefront of identifying potential demand for education and training. Work-based learning is seen as an essential aspect of the learning which underpins Foundation degrees and there has been some debate over the precise form that this should take but there has been a strongly articulated view that it should be firmly integrated into the award (not 'stand alone'), closely reflect the needs of the employment sector and constitute a 'genuine' (rather than 'token') experience of work in that particular occupational area. In terms of mode of delivery, the Foundation degree was articulated from the start as a response to those in work or wanting to enter work who required more flexible (open, distance, on-line and block release) forms of learning. Initial expectations of the appropriate social constituencies for Foundation degrees have, however, proved slightly wide of the mark and there has been a much more even divide between those studying part-time ('in work') and those involved in full-time study. The full-time/part-time distinction may, however, disguise much wider variations in programme design which rely, for example, on integrating work-based, on-line and 'blended' learning. The extent to which this and other forms of 'flexibility' have facilitated the widening of access to higher education, however, is still unclear given the deficiencies in the data which is available; it is likely though that, given the close correlation between lower socio-economic class and vocational study in the new universities and colleges of further and higher education, that Foundation degrees will be found to be serving these groups rather than the upper middle classes which cluster in the elite institutions (see Brennan 2002). This bears forcefully on the issue of progression since current signs are that a high proportion of those involved in Foundation degrees are progressing to a full honours degree even though this may not always be closely related to the employment focus or mode of study of their initial qualification.

Much of the above can (and has) been derived from policy documents and evaluations in the public domain. If properly interrogated these documents can 'tell a story' which – when linked to wider research on policy and practice – is indicative of the overall trajectory of Foundation degree development. Without much more in-depth, long-term and diversified research strategies, however, our knowledge of Foundation degrees will not go beyond these relatively simple limits. This would be disappointing. There is much which the community of Foundation degree practitioners and developers would like to know about the current state of the new qualification as evidenced by a recent *fdf* consultation on Foundation degree research which identified research priorities in terms of concerns as varied as work-based learning, employer engagement, student progression and recruitment, curriculum design and delivery, flexible and e-learning, development costs, data analysis, employability, full versus part-time provision, and patterns of supply and demand (Beaney 2005c). There are other research 'stories' which remain to be told and which go beneath these issues of design, development and delivery but nevertheless effectively underpin them. The latter, however, assumes a level of theorization and conceptualization which is, at the time of writing, largely missing.

The brief history of Foundation degrees outlined above has been accompanied by periodic attempts to investigate and evaluate the progress of the new qualification; primarily, but not exclusively, at the behest of government-sponsored organizations. Not all of these activities would be characterized by educational researchers as 'research' but I would argue that they have provided the practitioner community with a point of reference when other more formal forms of research have been unavailable. The main forms of investigation have been:

- government funded national evaluative studies by both private sector consultancies and academic researchers
- studies carried out as part of the QAA quality review process
- local and national surveys of provision sponsored by national and regional interest groups
- sectoral studies aimed at determining the extent and nature of existing provision vis-à-vis particular employment sectors
- regional studies of, for example, Foundation degree supply and demand
- practitioner research of pedagogic and practical issues to do with, for example, course design and delivery
- institutional studies of market supply and demand for particular sectors and subject areas
- professional studies of Foundation degree provision in specific areas of professional practice, e.g. early years education, health professionals.

Such a list seems quite extensive at first sight but there are rarely more than a few published examples in each category and the approaches and standards applied to each are very diverse. A few examples will suffice to illustrate this.

The first **QAA review of Foundation degrees** in 2003 gave us a fascinating snapshot of what had been happening to the first generation of Foundation degrees. It focused upon the distinctive features of the award, the quality of the student experience and whether programmes were meeting the standards set by the agency's benchmark statement. The review looked in detail at 33 individual Foundation degrees involving 3,100 students or one-third of the total number of students enrolled at the time of the review (QAA 2003). Out of this came a great deal of information regarding the then state of play with respect, for example, to work-based leaning, flexible delivery and the involvement of employers. However, because the reports on which the final overview was based were confidential we were not able to see the detail of each individual award. Thus, where QAA noted difficulties, for example, with respect to the implementation of work-based learning the lack of further detail leaves open questions about how these difficulties have arisen. Is it a question, for example, of work-based learning not being properly understood as a pedagogic approach or are there difficulties perhaps in engaging employers or students in the work place? Is there a need for professional development for staff working in this area in order to familiarize them with the pedagogic basis of work-based learning or is there rather a shortage of resources to support proper coordination of work and campus-based learning? These are issues about which we need more information if we want to know where to focus the efforts of the policy and practitioner community in terms of improving practice. The QAA review was not, of course, 'research'; it was evaluation from the point of view of quality assurance and there is necessarily a need for a level of confidentiality in seeking access to the detailed findings. However, the line between research and evaluation can be a very thin one. The QAA review involved a great deal of 'research', albeit for a particular purpose, and amassed a great deal of data and information which in an appropriately anonymised form would be useful to both researchers and practitioners. The most recent review, which took place in 2005, has both undertaken a more in-depth statistical and qualitative study of the total population of Foundation degrees and disseminated its results much more widely (see Amanda Nelson, this volume).

The second useful example of a major piece of evaluative 'research' is the recent **Taskforce Report on Foundation degrees**. Although this again was an evaluative exercise and not 'research' in the commonly accepted sense, it did draw upon various pieces of ongoing research which had been commissioned by HEFCE and which were able to give interim reports on the current state of the Foundation degree. The Taskforce was also able to draw upon other much wider and less structured information from a range of other sources including 'expert witnesses'. In this respect it mirrors much of what has happened in the sector to date in terms of evaluative research, which is that it drew necessarily quite heavily upon 'informed opinion'. It would be wrong to undervalue the latter in terms of some presumed 'harder' data. There is a role for professionally informed opinion alongside other research evidence of various kinds; especially when it involves access to the expert witnesses that many academic researchers would struggle to access. It provides moreover a form of rich qualitative evidence which is sometimes missing from quantitatively based surveys but has the drawback that it can easily mislead if informed opinion becomes accepted fact in the absence of other evidence. In the case of the Taskforce there was an opportunity to 'triangulate' but the evidence available to the Taskforce was inevitably partial and could ultimately only provide a snapshot, albeit a tantalizing one, of Foundation degree development.

These two examples give only an indicative idea of current 'investigations' regarding Foundation degrees but they do highlight the problems involved in achieving even a limited knowledge of the qualification and the nature of the activities (such as evaluation, monitoring and review) which, even though they may not be regarded as bona fide 'research', nevertheless provide starting points and ways into understanding Foundation degrees in the absence of other more systematic or apparently disengaged sources of information. Research, as has been relentlessly argued in recent years, is not a neutral activity and there is therefore no clear-cut distinction between different research domains such as 'pure' and 'applied' research. Research generally has some purpose, even if this is remote from the actual site of the research, and although the professional practices which surround research attempt to keep it free from, for example, overt bias there generally is an underlying perspective which can never be entirely eliminated. We can see this clearly if we look at the other forms of research activity which surround Foundation degrees. There are at least three other major sources of information worth mentioning.

The first is **data**, available from a wide range of institutional sources, which directly evidences the state of Foundation degrees in terms, for example, of student numbers, social and educational background, and forms of progression. The data on Foundation degrees is, however, very fragmented and dispersed in terms of the different agencies which collect data in this area. Information about Foundation degree students might, for example, be hidden in the catch-all survey category of 'other higher education' and HESA – the main source of data on higher education - does not include data relating to students studying Foundation degrees at further education colleges.

The second is at the opposite end of the spectrum and is the **practitioner or action based research** which has generally been undertaken by those involved in designing, delivering or developing Foundation degrees. This might include those based in various development and support agencies as well as those in educational institutions who are effectively researching their own practice. The latter is potentially a rich source of both information and enhanced practice but the limited financial and institutional support for practitioner research means that it is difficult to develop. Organisations such as *fdf* and the former LSDA (Learning and Skills Development Agency) have been engaged in supporting it and there have been various programmes which have provided support for those based, in particular, in further education, but there is still some way to go to meet even the modest levels achieved in recent years in higher education by organisations such as the former ILT (Institute for Learning and Teaching). This is not to say, however, that action research and evidence based practice have not been receiving increasing attention and growing in terms of both actual practice and professional recognition.

Finally, the area which might be expected to be most closely engaged with Foundation degree research, the formal **educational research community**, has to date given the new qualification very little attention. As noted above, there have been very few academically researched articles on Foundation degrees since their inception – although the number is gradually growing - and the formal research which has taken place has generally been funded by the DfES in relation to monitoring the progress of the Foundation degree initiative. This is a major omission and although it would be wrong to necessarily privilege formal academic research above other types there is clearly a role for it in providing a particular vantage point on Foundation degrees. Indeed, there is an argument for a range of different types of research which not only have different purposes but a range of links into both policy and practice. It is clear though that formal educational research is, as one recent review noted, heavily skewed towards certain types of education – particularly 'schooling' – and away from the much more recent innovations in open, distance, flexible, accessible and inclusive education (Silver 1999). The 'informal' and the 'vocational' are, therefore, not well served.

All of this points, I would argue, to the need for a range of different modalities of research regarding Foundation degrees which should complement and reinforce each other. An outline agenda for this forms the final part of this article. Before proceeding to this, though, we need to ask what can be learnt from existing 'research', in the broadest sense, into Foundation degrees:

- We know something of the history and trajectory of Foundation degree development from the now numerous official publications and evaluative reports which have characterized Foundation degree development. However, we know little of the experience of developers and institutions in terms of their engagement with Foundation degrees since no one has, to date, captured their experience or reflected upon its implications. The pace of Foundation degree development – particularly at the outset – has been very rapid and there has been limited opportunity for sustained reflection.

- We know something about the practices which programme teams and providers have entered into in order to establish Foundation degrees as a viable programme of study. The value of two QAA reviews is that there has been some systematic evaluation of Foundation degrees across a wide range of factors, even if this largely leaves aside other dimensions – such as widening participation – which are necessary for a fuller evaluation.

- The first QAA review of Foundation degrees didn't tell us a great deal about the detail of innovative practice within Foundation degrees since the full reports were not published. It did not tell us, for example, about where e-learning has worked and where it has not; about how PDP (Personal Development Planning) has been incorporated and whether it involves e-portfolios; about how providers interpret the QAA requirement for work-based learning to be treated as 'central' to Foundation degrees and whether or not simulation is an acceptable form of work-based learning; and it can't tell us how effective partnerships between educational providers, employers and other intermediaries can be achieved. We do know something about all of this from the attempts which have been made to gather and record evidence of good practice but much more needs to be done to make this an effective resource for the sector as a whole and to make what we know about Foundation degrees comparable with what we know about other sectors of education.

- We know something about the size and scope of Foundation degree provision, student numbers and background but there is very little comprehensive and systematic data. Foundation degrees are difficult to quantify because educational statistics cross institutional and sectoral boundaries, Foundation degree programmes are relatively unstable because of their emerging nature, and data sources are, therefore, fragmented and incomplete. Numbers with respect to Foundation degrees are thus frequently best guesstimates; a situation which needs to change if we are going to evaluate Foundation degrees - in relation to the objectives which have been set for them – on the basis of the best available evidence.

Why do research?

Much of the above inevitably leads us on to the question 'why do research?' The answer isn't as immediately obvious as we might like it to be and, as is well known, the question of the relevance of educational research to policy and practice has become a major policy issue. In the past it had almost been accepted wisdom that research would usefully feed into policy and practice debates if only indirectly through percolation rather than direct dissemination. This is no longer the case. There is now a very different and constrained environment for educational research in which funding is increasingly tied to particular and frequently practical outcomes (see, for example, the ESRC's Teaching and Learning Research Programme, TLRP). Whilst the debate on the relevance of educational research has been polarised and painful for some, I would argue that it has had the virtue at least of opening up questions about the value and practice of research which are of direct importance for Foundation degrees. Just as the latter challenge conventional approaches to learning by crossing organisational boundaries and involving employers in a process of collaborative course design the research which is required to support Foundation degrees will inevitably challenge intellectual orthodoxies since it is inherently interdisciplinary. Traditionally research in relation to learning and teaching has been heavily cognitive but in the case of Foundation degrees there are cross-cutting social and economic issues regarding, for example, the relationship between 'learning and earning', on the one hand, and widening social participation, on the other, which require an exploration of the interface between social and pedagogic research. More radically perhaps the advent of practitioner and action-based research as well as support for research located in further education colleges raises questions about the democratisation of research activity[9].

It is possible, then, that we might expect new and different things from research. We might expect research to be carried out in new locations and with different purposes. We might expect that the control over research and the funding for it be more devolved and applied (as, for example, in the former LSDA's commitment to supporting research in the learning and skills sector). We might expect that the boundaries between those engaged in, affected by and in receipt of research would become more blurred. Finally, we might expect that research could become more closely integrated with other procedural activities such as scholarship, quality enhancement and professional development. This is not just a wish list; there are signs that a different approach is emerging in response to the multiple pressures which arise from the changing demands on both the work place and the academy. Foundation degrees are themselves a response to such pressures since they attempt to articulate a vocational route through a largely non-vocationally orientated higher education system, for learners who might otherwise ignore further and higher education altogether.

What would it be valuable to know about Foundation degrees?

In conclusion, then, given the undeveloped state of Foundation degree research what would it be valuable to know about Foundation degrees if the will and the resources were there to find out?

Employer engagement

It would be valuable to know where, why and how employers have successfully engaged with the development and delivery of Foundation degrees. The fact that employers have been located at the heart of this process in design terms does not disguise the real difficulties which this engenders and the complex factors which influence engagement. Given the government's increasing desire to involve employers more centrally in setting objectives for education and training in their employment sectors as well as in actual delivery this is a key area for investigation.

Partnerships

We know an enormous amount now from economic sociology and elsewhere about how firms enter into partnerships across supply chains and which factors affect successful inter-firm partnerships but we know next to nothing about how employers successfully partner with educational institutions. One of the groundbreaking features of Foundation degrees has been their involvement of higher and further education providers together with employers in the process of course design and delivery. This socializes the learning process in ways which might be of use to other forms of learning which incorporate partnerships – e.g. in community and voluntary sector based learning – but we still know very little about the forms of mediation and negotiation as well as the contextualizing factors which underpin successful partnerships.

Work-based learning

Work-based learning is neither entirely new nor wholly innovative but its design and delivery within Foundation degrees raises, at a different level and on a larger scale, issues about the negotiation, implementation and successful support of learning in the work place. The relationship between learning and work is a very complex one and one which is also quite alien to the British educational tradition beyond private sector developments such as apprenticeships. Work-based learning poses particular challenges for all the educational partners since it requires them all to move beyond their accustomed environments and engage with educational processes which transgress traditional institutional and cultural boundaries.

Innovation

Foundation degrees have been linked with innovation and the close association with learners in full or part-time work means that innovative pedagogies have to engage with problems of multi-site delivery, the integration of academic and work-based learning, and the involvement of employers in many aspects of the learning process. Foundation degrees are, therefore, a testing place for many of the recent innovations in learning theory and practice. It is unclear, however, to what extent such innovations are being successfully adopted and how they impinge upon the learning cultures and experiences of learners. It is easy to assume that innovation will in, and of, itself be a 'good thing' but there is a good deal of evidence that suggests that 'top down' innovation which lacks an evidence base may ignore or distort the real needs of learners.

Progression

Foundation degrees are deeply implicated in the elaboration of new progression routes; an activity which characterizes contemporary education more generally. Foundation degrees are formally required to lead into Level 3 of an honours degree programme but they clearly may lead in many different directions – depending, for example, on professional requirements – and they also articulate, in terms of entry, with a range of other vocationally orientated qualifications (e.g. NVQs, vocational 'A' levels, and Advanced Modern Apprenticeships) as well as with prior experiential learning. We currently know very little about the key factors which influence learners in terms of making choices between different forms of provision at critical stages in their progression and where – if at all – they seek to step sideways or exit altogether from the educational process.

Data

We know something about the size and scope of Foundation degree provision, student numbers and educational background in broad terms but there is very little comprehensive and systematic data. Foundation degrees are difficult to quantify for the reasons noted above and because provision is still stabilizing. Numbers with respect to Foundation degrees are, therefore, frequently best guestimates; a situation which needs to change if we are going to evaluate Foundation degrees on the basis of the best available evidence. Unless these problems are clearly identified and represented to the data collection agencies we will never have a reliable data source to support research into Foundation degrees.

The above is simply a sample of some of the issues which might be addressed by a coherent research agenda and largely neglects the wider social issues which I have suggested need to be married to more conventional pedagogic concerns. In this chapter I have suggested that Foundation degrees have, in common with other forms of vocationally-focused education, received very little attention from the academic research community. Much of the research which is available has come from government or government funded bodies or from practitioners who have had to struggle with limited time, funding and resources to support research. There is nevertheless a great deal more happening than might at first appear if we adopt a more inclusive definition of research which embraces a wide range of 'scholarly and investigative activities': "People who see themselves as researchers may be full-time professionals in a university, independent organization or government body; or they may be researching as part of their work as teachers, managers or other professionals." (Morris and Norman 2004: section 1, p.1).

Foundation degrees, as already noted, almost inevitably challenge received wisdoms and generate new forms of practice and engagement. As also noted, however, any agenda needs to engage not only with the subject matter of research but also with its mode of operation if research is to become a more embedded activity. The challenging of the relevance of educational research, the resurgence of action research, and the new demands made by learners and employers on educational provision all require a rethinking of the role of research in the development process. At one level there needs to be coherent links between research, policy and practice; at another links need to be made between the scholarship of teaching, continuing professional development and practitioner based research. Increasingly the relationship between researchers (as research providers) and the consumers of research (practitioners as well as policy-makers) are being questioned and renegotiated. Important questions are being asked about how research is commissioned, carried out and reported on as well as the 'education' which funders and consumers need in order to identify and interpret research appropriate to their needs. At the same time, sectors of education which have previously been excluded from educational research – such as further education – are seeking to include it and integrate it with opportunities for professional development. Given, however, the time and resource constraints in further education it may only be through strategic collaborations with other institutions that this can be achieved. The emerging lifelong learning networks may well provide a focus for this. There are signs that such an agenda is being realized through diverse initiatives carried out by a range of agencies and individuals but if it is to have a coherent long-term future there needs to be stronger coordination, recognition and integration of these efforts. It would seem appropriate, then, that the radical innovations required for a successful implementation of the Foundation degree initiative should be accompanied by an inclusive and responsive approach to the role played by research and scholarship.

Notes:

[1] The views expressed in this chapter are those of the author and are not necessarily, therefore, those of *fdf* as an organisation.

[2] During the last two years I have, in addition to conventional literature searches, carried out a number of email based surveys and personal consultations with a view to identifying the 'grey literature' which exists about Foundation degrees. Some of this is accessible on the web but in other cases more local surveys and qualitative studies have not reached a wider audience. However, *fdf*'s journal, forward, has fulfilled a useful role by publishing reflective and evaluative research studies.

[3] Although there are no monographs on Foundation degrees there is a very useful edited collection of practitioner case studies: see Brennan and Gosling 2004.

[4] See Appendix 1 for a bibliography of research-based and scholarly publications relating to Foundation degrees.

[5] Foundation Degree Forward (*fdf*) held a conference in June 2005 entitled 'Researching Foundation degrees: constructing a national agenda' which directly addressed some of these issues as well as providing an opportunity to consult with the Foundation degree community regarding their priorities for Foundation degree research. Some of the material from this conference has been incorporated into this edited volume.

[6] The 'White Paper' referred to here is the white paper on higher education: *The Future of Higher Education* published in January 2003.

[7] Further education has recently been the subject of a government review, the Foster Review, and White Paper which have focused in part on the core issue of the role of further education in relation to other sectors of education.

[8] The government White Paper on higher education identified Foundation degrees as the main source of immediate expansion in higher education and further education, in association with an HEI (higher education institution), as the main provider of Foundation degrees.

[9] An example of this would be the Transforming Learning Cultures (TLC) in Further Education Project. This TLRP-funded project has focused on the relationship between research and learning cultures in further education. "The Project addresses three problems: (i) the need for a robust evidence base to support the enhancement of learning and teaching in FE; (ii) the need for deeper understanding of the nature of learning cultures, how they impact upon learning, and the means by which they can be transformed to enhance and improve learning; and (iii) the need to promote a system-wide research capacity in the FE sector and beyond." (Source: http://www.ex.ac.uk/sell/tlc/project2.htm)

References

Avis, J. et al (1996) *Knowledge and Nationhood: education, politics and work.* London: Cassell.

Avis, J. (2003) 'Post-compulsory education: issues for 16-18 year olds', in Bartlett, S. and Burton, D. (eds.) *Education Studies: essential issues.* London: Sage.

Beaney, P.W. (2005a) 'Researching Foundation degrees: making a case for the relevance of research', *forward,* Issue 4.

Beaney, P.W. (2005b) 'Researching Foundation degrees: turning research into practice', *Educational Developments,* Issue 6.2, May 2005.

Beaney, P.W. (2005c) 'Raising the Profile of Foundation degree Research: a report on *fdf*'s first national research conference', *forward,* Issue 7.

Brennan, J. (2002) 'Transformation or reproduction? Contradictions in the social role of the contemporary university', in Enders, J. and Fulton, O. (eds.) *Higher Education in a Globalising World.* Dordrecht: Kluwer Academic Publishers.

Brennan, L. and Gosling, D. (eds.) (2004) *Making Foundation Degrees Work.* Brentwood: SEEC

DfEE (2000) *Foundation Degrees: consultation paper.* Nottingham: DfEE.

DfES (2004) *Foundation Degree Taskforce Report to Ministers.* London: DfES.

Hammersley, M. (2002) *Educational Research, Policymaking and Practice.* London: Paul Chapman Publishing

Lea, J. et al (2003) *Working in Post-Compulsory Education.* Buckingham: Open University Press.

Longhurst, D. (2004) 'Foundation degree forward: research programme'. *forward,* Issue 2.

Morris, A. and Norman, L. (2004) *Collaborative Research in Practice.* Learning and Skills Centre Report.

QAA (2003) *Overview Report on Foundation Degree Reviews (conducted in 2003).* Gloucester: QAA.

QAA (2004). *Foundation Degree Qualification Benchmark.* Gloucester: QAA. Available at: http://www.qaa.ac.uk/reviews/foundationDegree/benchmark/FDQB.asp.

QAA (2005a) *Foundation degree qualification benchmark,* October 2004, QAA (065 10/2004). Gloucester: QAA. Available at:
http://www.qaa.ac.uk/reviews/foundationDegree/benchmark/FDQB.asp

QAA (2005b) *Report of a Survey to Follow Up Foundation Degree Reviews Carried Out in 2002-2003.* Gloucester: QAA.

Silver, Harold (1999) *Researching Education: themes in teaching-and-learning.* Bristol: Policy Press.

Young, M. (1993) 'A curriculum for the 21st Century? Towards a new basis for overcoming academic/vocational divisions', *British Journal of Educational Studies* v.41, n.3.

Young, M. and Spours, K. (1997) 'Unifying academic and vocational learning and the idea of the learning society', *Journal of Education Policy* v.12, n.6.

Chapter 2

Rethinking Research and Development

Andrew Morris
National Educational Research Forum

The problem

All of us involved in the improvement of education are fortunate to be 'living in interesting times'. Not only are programmes of reform at the very top of political agendas around the world, but there is also growing recognition of the difficulty of taking the right action. This is attracting attention to the question of *how*, as well as what, things are to be done. Analyses of policy options, evaluations of teaching strategies, studies of the effectiveness of systems abound. In the wake of this action and analysis, a serious concern is beginning to be expressed that compels us to reflect critically on the potential of social reform and of the sciences that underpin it. The concern is that although investments in education have significantly increased in many countries of the world and major changes have been wrought in the way schooling, pre-schooling, higher education and apprenticeships are organised, improvements in performance have not always matched them. For social policy this is a matter of the utmost concern, because educational opportunity is seen by many as one of the few routes for escaping the trap of poverty. Its importance for the future of social cohesion can hardly be exaggerated.

Against this backdrop, this chapter addresses the contribution of the "science base" to the improvement of education. It focuses, in particular, on current thinking and action on the role of the research and development (R&D) system: what we are learning about it and what we might try to do to improve it. Paradoxically, the case for emphasising the role of R&D is itself barely grounded in evidence, more perhaps in intuition. It is not easy to demonstrate that investment in R&D will result in commensurate improvements in educational performance. Arguments for such investment are based largely on analogies with other fields in which such investment has proved productive, or on individual cases or simply on personal belief.

Something like a movement appears to be developing around the issue of enhancing the use of R&D for public policy. Several tendencies are evident. First, a number of initiatives are developing around the world on evidence-informed approaches to policy and practice. In the UK leading roles are played in government by the cabinet office; in academe, by a number of research centres and programmes; and on behalf of practitioners, by many national agencies. Second, some have reacted to these initiatives by casting doubt on the possibility of accumulating educational knowledge in systematic ways and that R&D could ever yield the conclusive kind of information desired by decision-makers. An interesting study, undertaken recently by the National Research Council at the US National Academies of Science in Washington, addressed such doubts by considering the scientific basis of education. It concluded that the principles underlying scientific inquiry apply equally to education as to any other area (Shavelson and Towne, 2002). It offered six principles to bear this out.[1] My own view is that there is still some way to go before we could dismiss the possibility of a useful scientific contribution to decision-making in education. However, in this chapter I set aside these broader philosophical questions about the nature and potential of knowledge, interesting though they may be, in order to concentrate on thoughts about, and studies of, evidence-informed policy and practice.

The R&D system in education

Firstly, some characteristics of the R&D system itself. The word 'system' is chosen here to convey the idea of a set of connections and flows. The system includes the many kinds of organisations funding and carrying out research or development, but also the many kinds of organisations and individuals standing to benefit from it, as well as the parts that mediate between the two. Educational improvement commonly involves a complex interaction over time between teachers, leaders, officials, inspectors and advisers as well as developers and researchers; rarely is a problem simply identified, researched and addressed through direct implementation of recommendations. By using the system as the object of analysis we are able to move on from debating the perceived shortcomings of any one part – for example the academic, the practitioner-researcher or the government research manager – to holistic discussion of the efficacy of the entire programme of improvement.

Some kinds of difficulty are inherent in any system of R&D. First amongst these is the very connection between research and development. In many spheres, the need to improve a product or a service calls for development. Tools need to be refined; processes re-designed; people, skills and materials developed. In turn, development calls for research to advance understanding, release innovative thinking and test out ideas thrown up in the development process. In education, development activity is widespread (for example in college and school improvement activity, in materials development and in professional development programmes). High quality research also takes place in a number of centres. Rarely, however, are the two designed to inform or draw upon the other. Improvement initiatives may fail to take account of research findings and conversely research designs may fail to build on the outcomes of development work. Funding, phasing and prioritising are not coordinated between developmental and research bodies and the two communities have little opportunity to converse with one another. It may even be that the impulse to develop and change real world practices and the impulse to dissect and elaborate problems are, in some senses, at odds with one another. Perhaps that which motivates the development professional differs significantly from that which motivates a researcher. Productive interplay between the two has, nevertheless, heralded progress in many spheres of life and needs to be tested more thoroughly in education.

Greater interaction between research and development will not, however be achieved easily. It involves, increased understanding of other peoples' motivations, coordination of disparate funding and administrative procedures and joint planning processes. Beyond this lie perceptions of the differences in the esteem in which developers and researchers are held.

A further inherent difficulty for R&D is its relative dispensability during tough rounds of budget-cutting. It is a slow process, with delayed returns on investment. In times of stress, urgent pressures in the delivery of primary services inevitably outweigh pressure for R&D. Underfunding of R&D over the longer term, however, leads to a cumulative deficit in knowledge and understanding which can easily result in ill-founded and ineffective improvement strategies.

A particular weakness of R&D in education is the project-based, as opposed to programmatic, design of much activity. The project format enables complicated sets of activity to be packaged up and assigned objectives, resources and start- and end-dates. Such packaging ensures that R&D activity can be accommodated administratively within budgeting and scheduling procedures, alongside for example, purchasing of equipment and employment of staff. Desirable though this may be, it also has the effect of chopping up what might otherwise be sustained streams of activity and of downplaying uncertainties. A 'programme' architecture, in contrast, enables packages of activity to be set within a larger and more enduring framework. It does not require a predetermined timescale over the long term, nor precise specification of all that lies ahead. Through the passage of projects within a programme, it is possible to adjust priorities and re-set objectives in the light of earlier learning and the magnitude of transient funding. The ESRC Teaching and Learning Research Programme (TLRP) represents an example of such a framework: designed around long-term objectives, it has been able to grow in scale and adjust its focus consistently over its five years of existence.

Across education, despite many examples of excellent individual projects, we lack a coherent national R&D effort that addresses agreed priorities and produces an accumulating record of practical and theoretical outputs. In its place we have (with the exception of TLRP) a plethora of small scale, short term, disconnected activities. The interlinked contributions of research, policy development, implementation and institutional leadership cannot be realised because a programmatic notion of the whole does not exist. Timeframes are too short, leadership is not brought together, knowledge is not recognised as a cumulative good.

International perspective

Having sketched in a little of the pathology of the R&D system in the UK it is instructive, not to say relieving, to note how things stand internationally. It appears that many of the difficulties outlined above are experienced widely, at least within the countries of the OECD. A key report drafted in 1995 by Albert Tuijnman of the Netherlands and Maurice Kogan of the UK for the OECD Centre for Educational Research and Innovation, set out the problems starkly:

> "... the relatively low level of funding for educational R&D indicates doubt among policymakers and practitioners about the usefulness and relevance of such research ... this makes it difficult to raise additional funds. ... .While educational research ..... is best considered as an immature field, educational studies have nevertheless been undertaken for a long time. .... an equilibrium must be found between the consolidation and synthesis of existing knowledge and the development of new kinds of ideas and insights."
> (OECD, 1995, p.70)

As regards the relative quality of educational research in the UK, it appears, in broad terms, to be above average. The educational R&D system in England was praised (with some reservations) in a 2002 report by the OECD:

> "The quantity and quality of attention being paid to educational R&D ..... is remarkable, especially when contrasted to other nations . There is also a "high degree of sophistication in the capacity of British social science to provide definitive evidence." (OECD, 2002, p.7)

The same report indicated that expenditure on R&D as a proportion of turnover, of the order of 0.5%, was very low in comparison with other knowledge industries, but perhaps a little above the average of several OECD countries.

With this overall picture of a fragmented, under-funded R&D system facing many difficulties, but performing reasonably well by international comparisons, I now turn to consideration of reform of the current arrangements.

Reform: the case for change

An initial question is: what would an improved system of R&D be for? For some it is self-evident that research and development improve people's lives. They have transformed the natural sciences from what was once a disinterested quest for understanding to the engine of technological, and hence economic, progress. In education, the proposition is that teachers and institutional leaders would make better judgements about their practice were it to be informed by research knowledge. Policy would be the better for it too.

At the present time, however, there is limited evidence to show this to be true. Yet decision-makers at school, college and university level and in government need more than fine words to be persuaded. Would they really be advised to divert attention from more immediate demands, to slow down their decision-making to allow time to study research evidence? In a number of honourable cases, this is indeed what happens and benefits are made apparent for all to see. In the main, however, arguments for evidence-informed decision-making in education currently appeal more to belief than evidence.

Yet many, including some in influential positions, hold firmly to this belief. A powerful example was expressed by the education ministers of the OECD countries in 1990 when they met and issued a communiqué declaring that:

> "The potential of educational research as an integral element of improvement remains largely underdeveloped .... In general the level of investment is far lower than in any other sector of comparable size .... much research needs to be grounded in practice, involving staff and institutions .... in a constant process of diagnosis, comparison and analysis."
> (OECD, 1995, p.9)

At an OECD conference on linking evidence to practice in 2005, 10 years after this report, one of its authors was dismayed to note how little the agenda for discussion had changed despite ten years of activity. Undoubtedly there have been important developments in the production and exploitation of R&D, such as the growth of systematic reviewing, but some remain mired in controversy and most still contribute little to the hurly-burly of actual educational delivery.

So the case for reform can hardly be made on the basis of systematic evidence. It relies more on appeal to analogies with fields that have moved in the evidence-informed direction and on the intuition of individuals and organisations that better decisions would be made were research evidence to be used more frequently, and that substantive improvements in learning would occur as a result of this.

In England a number of important developments occurred during the late 1990s and early 2000s in response to weaknesses in the relation of evidence to policy and practice. The incoming 1997 labour government set in train actions which led to a major report on the state of the educational R&D (Hillage et al, 1998). Several recommendations from this report were acted upon, leading to the creation of a National Educational Research Forum (NERF), a centre for research synthesis (the Evidence for Policy and Practice Information and Co-ordinating Centre - EPPI) and a number of new dedicated research centres, all funded by government. The 2002 OECD examination of the educational R&D system in England lent powerful support to these initiatives. Reflections on the experience of one of them, the National Educational Research Forum, forms the core of the following section.

The case of NERF

The National Educational Research Forum was specifically created to address strategic weaknesses in the UK educational R&D system. Constituted in 1999 as a forum, a place for talking together, rather than as an executive body, NERF brought together many of the disparate elements of the fragmented community identified in the Hillage report. Its members identified underlying themes that bound them together and debated differences in their points of view. In its early phase, working parties met, reports were produced and seminars held. It moved on to develop concise strategic proposals, consulted with government and others (Smith and Feuer, 2002) and made proposals to the Secretary of State. In essence these stated that serious improvement would require radical change. In particular, a national centre was needed in which evidence would be brought together, transformed for use and acted upon with the practice and policy communities. Further, to provide reliable, relevant and useful evidence, programmes that combine development and research (D&R programmes) would be needed that engage the people who effect actual change at classroom, institutional and policy levels as well as researchers.

Whilst these proposals were under consideration by political leaders, a number of projects were launched involving organisations and individuals eager to make advances. There was widespread frustration with the low impact of research evidence on the improvement of practice and with the inadequacies of a poorly connected R&D system. This led to active collaboration amongst universities, schools, colleges, government-linked agencies, and teacher organisations to develop and test the two proposals. I offer here two or three examples of this collaborative project work.

The Training and Development Agency for Schools (formerly the Teacher Training Agency) and the General Teaching Council for England wished to develop an internet portal to search and find evidence on topics of interest to teachers and trainers. Because this proved of interest to many other organisations, others joined the project. The group is currently addressing questions of categorising knowledge, defining quality, reaching sources and satisfying user needs. A pilot version is under development, sponsored by the software industry.

The proposal for a national centre of evidence has recently been elaborated by a working party of the National Educational Research Forum. With the participation of teachers, academics and policymakers and expertise from the social and health care fields, the working party has recently set out a specification for consideration. It covers the gathering and selection of research evidence, the publication of syntheses and guidance material for practitioners and policymakers and the support for networks of people to help make use of the material.

In relation to the concept of D&R programmes, NERF has set up a network of organisations and individuals who believe D&R programmes are important and are already experimenting with some aspect of them. It has also established two short life working groups with teacher, researcher and policymaker inputs, to devise plans for D&R programmes on pressing issues: student behaviour and physical science and maths education. Such programmes are conceived as a process of iteration between systematic study and practical development aiming to improve understanding at both classroom and theoretical levels. They involve many projects or units of activity and draw on a wide range of disciplinary inputs. Teachers, lecturers and decision-makers participate alongside researchers on terms of mutual esteem.

The expectation of a D&R programme is that teachers, lecturers, researchers and policy-linked people will form an agreement on key issues to attend to, create mechanisms for communicating with one another and get started on both developmental activity and on investigations of key questions. Although broad aims are to be agreed in advance, tactical options are expected to be adjusted as the work progresses, in the light of interim findings. Development is expected to throw up questions for careful research, and research to give rise to the development of tools or ways of thinking. Iterations between development and research activity will be a distinguishing feature of the programmes and will call for high level communication between the parties and perhaps a free-standing programme management or brokerage function.

The NERF network is currently addressing some of the challenges presented by these ideas: who would be likely to invest for several years in an untested design? How can short-term action be integrated with longer term scholarly study? How will teachers find time to participate?

Two related studies commissioned by NERF recently investigated the readiness of teachers to participate in programmes of development and research. Schools and further education colleges that already encourage teacher research were identified (Barker, 2005). Interviews with key personnel suggested that there is an appetite for such engagement, at least in some schools and colleges, but that funds would need to be made available for the release of teachers and coordination of activity (Rickinson, 2005).

In summary, the core proposals from NERF are for integrated programmes of development and research, contributing new useable knowledge to a national evidence centre. But how could such radical changes be brought about? The proposals themselves are contested and the changes they imply for funding and organisation will undoubtedly meet with resistance. But, at the same time, pressure to try out such approaches arises due to the persistent frustration felt by many about the failure of systematically acquired knowledge to impinge sufficiently on professional practice. Because of the profound nature of the struggle between these two tendencies, my own belief is that the changes required will take a long time to come about – more at the pace of cultural than of political change. Steady incremental steps in the right direction are a more likely prospect than rapid or dramatic changes.

Conclusions

Six years after the Hillage report that gave rise to NERF and the EPPI centre, and 10 years after the 1995 OECD report on educational R&D, what have we learned? First it is clear that the lofty ambitions of these reports have not been realised, at least in full. The aspirations have turned out to be difficult to act upon in a field where purposes are muddled, methodologies underdeveloped and world views contested. The Hillage report itself expressed doubts about its own recommendations, the authors themselves declaring initial uncertainty as to whether a National Educational Research Forum would work.

If evidence initiatives have failed to produce the concrete improvements originally hoped for, could this simply be the result of shortcomings in the way they were designed or carried out? My own belief, with the benefit of hindsight, is that although this may be part of the problem, the greater part is that the original expectations may have been unrealistic. The experience of bringing people together from the domains of policy, practice and research in recent years has brought into the open significant, underlying differences in the cultures within which they work and the obstacles to collaboration that these give rise to.

An alternative interpretation of the slow pace of progress of evidence initiatives, such as NERF, is that perhaps the wrong starting point was chosen for reform. Perhaps it is not research itself that should have been the priority for attention, but rather the system to which it contributes. Perhaps reform of the *demand* for evidence should be addressed before the supply side? As the senior economist at the European Investment Bank, Albert Tuijnman, pointed out in a speech to an OECD 2005 conference *Linking Evidence to Practice*, there are markets for knowledge and they do not appear to be working effectively in education. Knowledge has value and therefore should have a price at which supply can meet demand. If weaknesses in the R&D system in education are the result of weak demand, it may be that those who actually need it are failing to express, or perhaps even feel, the need. With important exceptions, practitioners are not calling vociferously for a research base to inform their daily work. Policymakers, though calling for items of evidence as the occasion arises, have not yet demanded an ongoing base from which evidence might be drawn. Little demand has been expressed in the past, through the professional development apparatus surrounding teaching. Neither teacher training, CPD nor inspection processes have raised strong expectations that research evidence should be used. Likewise, processes for decision-making in government and other policy organisations, moving as they do at a swift and jolting pace, mean that officials necessarily make do with whatever evidence is to hand – research-based or otherwise.

Given such realities in the way research is actually used, what can be said about how to cultivate demand for systematically acquired knowledge in the future? First, evidence from both research and practice need to be developed in relation to the difficult, persistent issues that underlie the delivery of learning, rather than in reaction to transient policy initiatives. Such evidence needs to be accumulated and made available for use on an ongoing, rather than a reactive, basis. This alone would represent a huge advance. To achieve it, existing evidence would first have to be selected and reviewed and conclusions and implications drawn. The D&R programmes would need to designed and funded that built on this and elaborated and extended it cumulatively, in ways that would prove useful for practice.

Second, changes in teaching and policymaking cultures would need to be brought about, at a pace and over a timescale, suited to cultural change. For evidence to be effectively used on a large scale, practitioner time would need to be allocated for the purpose and the intermediary organisations that stand between practice and research would themselves need to model evidence-using behaviour. Inspectorates, intervention programmes, leadership practices and professional development processes, for example, would need to make use of research evidence themselves as a prelude to building in an expectation of others. Third, as the demand for research evidence began to develop, new programmes of D&R would be needed to extend insight and develop tools in the areas where the cupboard is currently bare.

Notes:

[1] Six scientific principles: a committee was set up by the National Research Council of the National Academies in Washington to consider the scientific basis for education. Its report (Shavelson and Towne, 2002, p2) concludes that "six guiding principles underlie all scientific inquiry, including educational research:

1. pose significant questions that can be investigated empirically
2. link research to relevant theory
3. use methods that permit direct investigation of the question
4. provide a coherent and explicit chain of reasoning
5. replicate and generalise across studie
6. disclose research to encourage professional scrutiny and critique"

To put these principles in context the report goes on to say (p.5) that in addition to these common principles "every field of study develops a specialisation as the principles are applied..........education has its own set of features that give rise to the specialisation of educational research....education is multilayered, constantly shifting and occurs within an interaction among institutions, communities and families. It is highly value laden and involves a diverse array of people and political forces that significantly shape its character. These features require attention to the physical, social, cultural and economic and historical environment in the research process...".

References

Barker, P. (2005) *Research in Schools and Colleges.* NERF Working Paper no.7.2.

Hillage, J. et al (1998) *Excellence in Research on Schools.* Research Briefing RR7, London: DfES.

OECD (1995) *Educational Research and Development: Trends, Issues and Challenges.* Paris: OECD.

OECD (2002) *Educational Research and Development in England. Examiners report.* Available from CERI, Paris.

Rickinson, M. (2005) *Practitioners' Use of Research.* NERF Working Paper no 7.4.

Shavelson, R. and Towne, L. (2002) *Scientific Research in Education.* Washington: National Academy Press.

Smith, M. and Feuer, M. (2002) *Review of NERF Proposals.* NERF Working Paper no. 3.2.

2

Quantitative and Qualitative Approaches

Chapter 3

Provision and Participation:

USING QUANTITATIVE RESEARCH TO EXPLORE FOUNDATION DEGREE PROVISION

Amanda Nelson
Quality Assurance Agency

Introduction

Recent years have seen a variety of research within the UK in respect of Foundation degrees in relation to their aims, development and quality. However, there has been little statistical information available to stakeholders, including the higher education sector, regarding the national context of Foundation degree provision and participation within the higher education sector.

Given the vocational nature of Foundation degrees and their positioning at the intermediate stage on the skills level, their link with the market place and market forces is inextricable. However, little is known about the provision of Foundation degrees by programme (subject) in relation to the local labour market areas or other regional economic factors. A recent series of papers in the *fdf* forward journal (*fdf*, 2005) has sought to shed some light on regional provision of Foundation degrees in relation to the local labour market and sector skills classifications. The QAA, as part of its 2004-05 Reviews of Foundation degrees, additionally sought to consider the extent to which both Sector Skills Councils and local employers had been involved in the design, development and review of Foundation degree programmes and their contribution to student teaching and learning, in relation to local skills needs (QAA, 2005a).

There is currently a relative paucity of information and research pertaining to provision and participation in Foundation degrees in the UK. Information currently available from sources such as HESA suggests that there has been steady growth in the number of students enrolled on Foundation degrees (HESA, 2005a) since their introduction.

One of the defining characteristics of Foundation degrees lies in their core aim of widening participation and providing a route for those from non-traditional backgrounds to develop both academic and vocational skills through entry into higher education (DfES, 2003; QAA, 2005c; Wilson et al, 2005; Rowley, 2005). To date, there has, however, been no comprehensive analysis of the extent to which recruitment has met the expectations of the widening participation agenda. There is some evidence that Foundation degrees are recruiting students from non-traditional qualification backgrounds but little evidence as to students' socio-demographic and economic characteristics. Although there is evidence that the introduction of the Foundation degree award has created new opportunities for providers to offer more vocationally orientated higher education programmes (QAA, 2005c; Little, 2005).

In the light of the paucity of an appraisal of the national context of Foundation degrees, there is considerable scope for research into provision and participation. Given the relative newness of the award, longitudinal analysis of participation and progression has not previously been possible, but as additional cohorts complete and progress on to articulated awards or return to the work place, there will be greater opportunities available to the researcher to consider student characteristics and throughput data.

Not all research into Foundation degrees has been restricted to statistical information. Case study research has sought to consider direct student experience, and the experience of employers (Little, 2005) and providers of Foundation degree programmes (*fdf,* 2005). Although it is evident that case study based research is taking place, little has been formally published. The recent QAA reviews of Foundation degree programmes have generated a wealth of intelligence in relation to the development and design of Foundation degree programmes, quality and standards of provision, and emerging good practice with regards to academic standards and the student learning experience (QAA, 2005a, b,c).

There is currently a wide range of stakeholder interest with regard to Foundation degree programmes. Each of the stakeholder groups has its own agenda and information needs. This has led to a variety of largely uncoordinated investigations, much of which has been to fulfil the requirements of individual stakeholders and has not been shared or published. This is not, however, to be over-critical: such information as these studies have provided inevitably aids local providers understand both the local market (potential students' and employers' needs), and provides a national context for decision-makers and policy-makers in respect of planning for the future and monitoring and evaluating current policy and provision.

Nonetheless, for serious progress to be made a more co-ordinated approach to research and information is necessary if we are to increase our understanding of a variety of aspects of Foundation degrees as a whole. Additionally, it can provide a mechanism for monitoring and evaluation in line with national higher education agendas, whilst maintaining a watchful eye on quality and standards. Information is useful to providers at the local level as well as national organisations with a vested interest in Foundation degrees.

The aim of this chapter is to place Foundation degree provision and participation in context.

It seeks to provide a brief overview of provision and participation in Foundation degrees, focusing upon:

- data and information
- provision and participation
- students' characteristics
- emerging research questions.

Data and information

HESA collects a wide array of information pertaining to students in higher education within the UK, to include Foundation degree students, through the HESA student record. HESA collects data relating to indirectly funded provision (that provision where those students enrolled on Foundation degree programmes are done so through the awarding higher education institution). The Learning and Skills Council collects information regarding students enrolled on directly funded programmes.

There is currently no directly comparable set of data regarding students enrolled on Foundation degree programmes, as the funding routes determine the statistical returns. This has been a contributory factor to the current paucity of research and information at the national level with regards to the overall picture of Foundation degrees. The lack of research can also, as noted previously, be partially attributed to the lack of sufficient cohort data, while the position is further complicated for both researchers and policy-makers by the fact that different collectors of data employ different terminology and classification structures.

Brown (2005) demonstrated from studies within the South West significant information gaps in relation to Foundation degrees, and suggested that such information gaps render further education colleges, HEIs (higher education institutions), employers and other decision-makers badly placed to develop judgements on Foundation degree provision, and also lead to unhelpful or non-existent press coverage of Foundation degree initiatives (Brown 2005: 11).

Another information source is yielded by the efforts of agencies and organisations in gathering relevant information pertaining to provision and participation to meet their own requirements. UCAS (Universities & Colleges Admissions Service) holds a wealth of data regarding applications and acceptances for Foundation degree programmes, but again this is not a complete national set of data. *fdf* has compiled a composite data set relating to all the provision of all Foundation degree programmes, both current and proposed (*fdf* 2005). In essence, not only are additional cohort data becoming available for analysis, but also a greater number of agencies and organisations are becoming involved in Foundation degrees and are subsequently collecting previously untapped data, which lends itself to research and interrogation. This further suggests the need for stakeholders to work together and align both their information requirements and research activities.

In analysing participation and provision data it is additionally useful to analyse it comparatively against other data sets, and consider other causal influences and factors. For example, a review of progression and withdrawal rates for Foundation degree students suggests relatively high rates of withdrawal. However, these should be interpreted in respect of other socio-demographic factors and benchmarked against withdrawal and progression rates for similar awards at the same intermediate level of the FHEQ (Framework for Higher Education Qualifications) or NQF (National Qualifications Framework), for example HNDs/HNCs if they are to be meaningful.

Currently, the progression of Foundation degree students through and following their programme of study can only be tracked through the fussy matching of data sets, making longitudinal analysis of Foundation degree students challenging. Formal longitudinal analysis allows for an analysis of enrolments and completions, and provides evidence in respect of widening participation and added value for students/individuals following successful completion. However, as more cohorts complete there is a greater volume of post-completion data available, be it employment or progress onto an honours degree. This information can be derived from an analysis of the HESA student record and the HESA Destination of Leavers in Higher Education survey. HESA is therefore an important collector of information about Foundation degree students.

Provision and participation

Growth in provision

Recent years have seen a significant growth in the provision of Foundation degree programmes and delivery sites. Information from HESA (2005b) suggests that there was around a 23% increase in the number of awarding institutions offering Foundation degrees programmes between 2002-03 and 2003-04. Additionally, between 2002-03 and 2003-04, there was a 72% increase in the number of delivery sites through which Foundation degrees were delivered (HESA 2005b). This growth was further demonstrated through the QAA Foundation degree Scope and Preference Exercise (QAA 2004). This revealed that in 2002-03 just under 200 programmes were offered on 241 delivery sites, but that by 2003-04 these figures had increased to over 400 programmes offered through over 550 delivery sites (QAA 2004), a 117% growth in programmes and a 133% growth in the number of delivery sites.

Growth in participation

HESA (2005a) has stated that in 2003-04, over 21,000 students were registered on Foundation degree programmes within England, Wales and Northern Ireland. Of these, 64% were in their first year of study. There was a recorded growth of 62% in first year entrants between 2002-03 and 2003-04, and an overall growth of 91% in respect of total enrolments (HESA, 2005a and b). Enrolments on Foundation degree programmes are currently growing at a greater rate than any other UK higher education award.

The continued growth in Foundation degree recruitment is further demonstrated through the UCAS applications data for 2005. As of March 2005, over 24,000 applications for Foundation degree study for 2005-06 had been received by UCAS (UCAS, 2005). The UCAS data showed a 160% increase in applications for study in 2003-04 to 2005-06. However, between 2003-04 and 2004-05 UCAS reported a 79% increase in applications and a 58% increase in acceptances (UCAS 2005). This suggests that demand appears to be growing at a faster rate than availability of places. Patterns of increase additionally displayed a geographical dimension (see Figure 1).

The HESA data (HESA 2005a) illustrate that over a comparable period (2002-03 to 2003-04), whilst there was a 62% growth in the number of entrants onto Foundation degree programmes there was a decline of 19.6% and 9.2%, respectively, in the numbers enrolled on HNDs and HNCs. The QAA Scope and Preference exercise highlighted the fact that around one-third of Foundation degree programmes on which students were enrolled in 2003-04 had been converted from a HND or HNC to a Foundation degree programme (QAA 2004). It is useful to note that patterns emerged with regards to subject clusters of HND/HNC programmes converted to Foundation degrees (QAA 2004). Education, the largest and one of the most rapidly growing areas of provision, was not a subject area where HND/HNCs had converted into Foundation degree programmes. Conversions appeared to be clustered among more 'technically' orientated programmes (QAA 2004).

The additional funded Foundation degree places allocated through the outcomes of the HEFCE funding bid (HEFCE 2004) are likely to contribute to the continued future growth of Foundation degree programmes. The outcomes of the bid confirmed the allocation of a total of 7,185 new places (5,211 FTE full-time equivalent) at Foundation degree level for 2004-05. Full-time places accounted for 2,524 of the total, and the remaining 4,661 places (2,687 FTE) were for part-time programmes. For 2005-06 a total of 5,013 new places (3,749 FTE) were allocated with full-time places making up 2,133 of the total with the remaining 2,880 places (1,616 FTE) being for part-time provision. These additional funded places had both regional and subject dimensions.

Nonetheless, these figures are not so straightforward as they might initially appear. While in 2003-04, 80 HEIs in England offered Foundation degree programmes, three such institutions, each of which recorded over 1,000 registered Foundation degree students, accounted for 14% of all enrolled Foundation degree students – an important fact to bear in mind when considering both the geographical distribution of programmes, and growth trends in programmes and student enrolments.

Increase in UCAS applications for Foundation degrees (2003-2005)

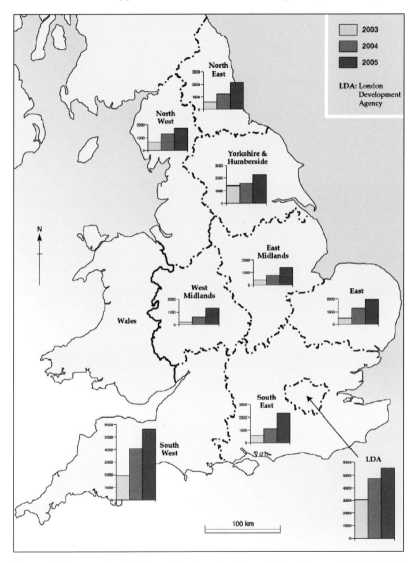

Figure 1: Increase in UCAS applications for Foundation degrees (2003-2005)

Source: UCAS Note: 2005 Application data as at May 2005

Subject/programme of study

In 2002-03 and 2003-04, Education recorded the greatest number of student enrolments, and the greatest rate of growth (HESA 2005a). In 2003-04 around one-third of all Foundation degree students in the UK were enrolled on Education programmes (see Figure 2).

Despite the fact that Creative Arts and Design recorded only the fourth largest number of student enrolments in 2003-04, it recorded the greatest number of qualifiers (HESA 2005c). This opens the possibility of a shift in the subject-orientated profile of Foundation degree programmes in respect of the recent (numerical) growth in Education and Business and Administration enrolments. Enrolments on Education programmes have grown at a faster rate than the total number of Foundation degree enrolments. Proportionally, other subject areas have experienced a relative decline in their market share, despite increases in absolute numbers.

Inevitably, the additional HEFCE funded student places will have a future impact upon student enrolments at the subject level, especially in respect of Education and Business and Administration.

Subject of Study (HESA)

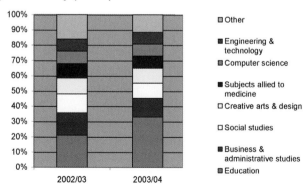

Figure 2: Breakdown of Foundation degree students by subject
Source: HESA 2005a

54

When considering subjects studied it is useful to note the various classifications used. The information collected by HESA in relation to subject of study is classified on the basis of JACS (Joint Academic Coding System). This academic coding bears no direct relationship to the sector skills classification that is also used as a method of classifying provision. The point is not that either is deficient: on the contrary both can be considered appropriate given the intended academic and vocational skills integration which is a central feature of Foundation degrees. But given that other agencies involved in Foundation degrees, for example QAA, also employ their own subject classification system, attempts at triangulation and analysis of the data are unavoidably impaired. Consideration needs, therefore, to be given to the classification used in research into provision and participation, especially when considering local labour market areas, employment or vocational factors.

Geographical characteristics

There are evident geographical patterns in respect of Foundation degree provision within England. In some regions limited opportunities exist for study on a Foundation degree programme. During 2003-04, London, the South East and the South West offered the greatest number of Foundation degree programmes within England (QAA 2004), and reported the greatest number of student enrolments (HESA, 2005b) (see Figures 3 and 4, Table 1). Two of the primary providers of Foundation degrees within the UK are based within the South East and South West, though a good part of the reason for the South East's domination lies in the student numbers enrolled through the Open University.

Conversely the North East, Yorkshire and Humberside and the West Midlands offered the fewest programmes and report fewer enrolled students. These geographical inequalities of Foundation degree provision persist – even when controlling for such external factors as population density.

HESA data confirm that the three regions that experienced the greatest growth in Foundation degree enrolments between 2002-03 and 2003-04 were:

- West Midlands – 132%
- South West – 113%
- North West – 101%

However, despite the West Midlands displaying the greatest growth rate, the numbers involved were relatively small, and interpretation of regional patterns on the basis of rates of growth detracts from true regional growth trends.

Regional Development Agency	% Foundation degree students	First year Foundation degree enrolments 2003-04
South West	18%	19%
South East	17%	18%
London	17%	17%
North West	16%	15%
East	9%	8%
East Midlands	7%	7%
Yorkshire and the Humber	6%	7%
West Midlands	6%	7%
North East	5%	4%

Note: all percentages have been rounded to the nearest integer.

Table 1: Students registered on Foundation degrees by region (2003-04)
Source: HESA 2005b

Delivery site by region (%)

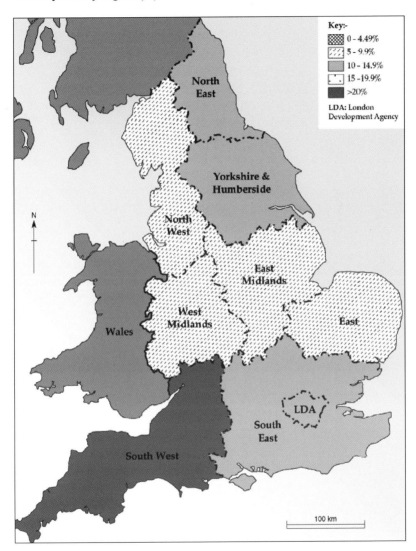

Figure 3: Delivery site by region (%)

Source: QAA Scope and Preference Exercise, 2004

Students registered on Foundation degrees, by region (2003-2004)

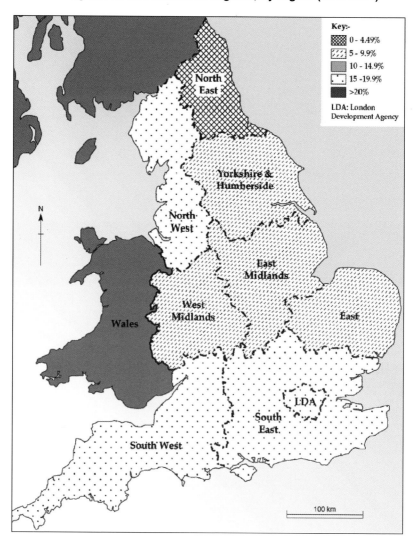

Figure 4: Students registered on Foundation degrees, by region (2003-2004)

Source: HESA 2005

The allocation of additional HEFCE funded Foundation degree places introduces a spatial component, accentuating regional variations in provision and participation. The largest number of applications for additional places was received from the South West and London, currently two areas with the majority of Foundation degree programmes and levels of participation. However, in terms of the successful applications for 2004-05 and 2005-06 additional places, these were allocated to London, the South East and Yorkshire and Humberside. Those areas with additional funded places are therefore likely to display the greatest rates of growth. London and the South East currently have a high percentage of the Foundation degree enrolments, with the allocation of additional HEFCE funded places, the spatial inequalities in respect of provision (or the gap between highest and lowest) will become even further pronounced. Additionally, this may place greater pressure upon honours degree places should students choose to articulate, unless there is comparable growth in the availability of honours degree places. As little is known at present about progression onto articulated awards, however, it is not currently possible to estimate the extent of this pressure.

There are notable geographical variations in respect of the subject of study. HESA data show that three regions alone accounted for over two-thirds of all enrolments within Education (65%), with almost two-thirds of all Foundation degree students enrolled in the South East being on Education programmes – a figure significantly distorted, however, by the fact that over half of those students were enrolled with the Open University, irrespective of where they lived.

The North West recorded the second greatest number of enrolments of Education Foundation degree programmes, by region, with such students accounting for over a quarter (27%) of all Foundation degree students enrolled within the region. Education related programmes were offered primarily through four awarding HEIs. Similarly, a quarter (25%) of all Foundation degree students enrolled in the South West were on Education programmes. However, this provision was offered almost exclusively through one awarding HEI, with over three-quarters (75%) of the students being taught directly through the awarding HEI.

It is apparent that in respect of both current provision and planned future growth there are spatial inequalities in terms of equivalence of opportunity. Opportunities to enrol on Foundation degree programmes, especially full-time programmes, appear to be heavily influenced and even, in some cases, determined, by domiciliary location. However, there is also evidence from the QAA Foundation degree Reviews that many Foundation degree programmes have a national rather than purely local or regional market (QAA 2005c). This was deemed to be a characteristic of some professionally focused part-time programmes, where sites of work-based learning were outside of the immediate geographical area of the provider, but spatially aligned with where the student lived and worked. The geographical market place of Foundation degree programmes is another under-researched area of provision.

Nor is distance necessarily a limiting factor in respect of access to Foundation degree programmes. Around one in 10 Foundation degree programmes contain a distance or e-learning element, and 3% of Foundation degree programmes were delivered entirely through distance or e-learning methods (QAA 2004). Though currently small, trends elsewhere in the higher education sector suggest that they are more likely to increase than to decrease over time.

Little formal evidence currently exists regarding those factors that act as the stimuli for the development of Foundation degree programmes locally, in particular as to the nature of the interplay between local employment needs and demand from potential local students. It is not known, therefore, whether this acts as a catalyst for the development of Foundation degrees or whether the stimulus comes from the awarding institution itself, either through the identification of a potentially untapped market, or through existing specialist academic provision within a sector/subject area. There is, however, some evidence (Rowley 2005) that skills needs as suggested by regional development agencies, and Sector Skills Councils constitute one factor informing curriculum development (Rowley 2005: 10).

In respect of the notion of the 'geographical sphere of influence' or 'market area' of Foundation degrees, anecdotal evidence collected through the QAA Foundation degree Reviews (QAA 2005c) suggests that there are three main types of Foundation degree programme. On this basis, an embryonic typology of Foundation degree programmes can be suggested. It is apparent that the majority of Foundation degree programmes recruit from the local market area; full-time programmes are typically of this type. These can be considered as Type 1: Local. A second group of programmes are those that have a wider geographical area and offer a professional qualification embedded within the programme; these are specialist programmes and are offered on a part-time or full-time basis. These can be considered as Type 2: National (professional). The third group of Foundation degree programmes are those that are specialist and align with a specific employment sector, and have a national recruitment market. These are typically part-time and can occasionally be undertaken through distance or distributed learning routes, whilst students continue in full-time employment. The work-based learning aspect of these are generally through the existing employer, and located outside of the immediate geographical region of the provider. This third type can be considered as Type 3: National (specialist). However, qualitative research would be necessary to further explore the emergence of a possible typology of Foundation degrees.

Student profile

Foundation degrees aim to widen participation through encouraging students who otherwise may have elected not to do so, to enter higher education (DfES 2003; QAA 2005a, b, c; Rowley 2005). Hence they are designed to provide a route into higher education for students who did not previously do so as a result of a complex interplay of choice and constraint mechanisms. The findings of the 2004-05 QAA Reviews of Foundation degree programmes suggested that in relation to widening participation, there is evidence to demonstrate a commitment to widening participation through recruitment, and that in many cases admissions procedures accommodate accreditation of prior (experiential) learning as an alternative 'qualification' for entry (QAA 2005c).

However, an analysis of the socio-demographic characteristics of students enrolled on Foundation degree programmes reveals a dualism. This dualism is evident in respect of new enrolments on Foundation degrees from 2001-02 through to 2004-05, and has been confirmed through an analysis of both the HESA student data and data collected by QAA in support of the recent Foundation degree Review activities .

Two distinct, though not entirely mutually exclusive, clusters emerge on the basis of student characteristics and mode of learning. The first predominantly comprises males aged 25 years or under, who entered the Foundation degree programme directly from education or training, possessed 'A' level GCE/VCE qualifications as their highest recorded qualification on entry, and were enrolled on full-time programmes. The second cluster is of similar size but predominantly comprises females, aged 26 years and over, studying on a part-time basis who entered the Foundation degree programme from employment or other non-educational/training activities and were less likely to possess any academic or vocational qualifications.

It has been shown previously that during periods of economic expansion women are more likely to return to the work place, but that at times of recession they are liable to be squeezed out before male employees. As such, it is a reasonable preliminary hypothesis that women are using Foundation degree programmes as a route for returning to the work place, and their enrolment is directly related to the current period of relative economic buoyancy. Conversely, Foundation degrees, due to their flexible nature, may present opportunities for mature female students who have previously been prevented from doing so due to choice and lifestyle constraints to enter education, while males are using Foundation degrees as a route onto an honours degree programme. It is only through the analysis of post completion activity that this hypothesis as to the relationship between demographic (including gender) and lifestyle characteristics on the one hand and purpose or motivation for undertaking a Foundation degree programme on the other can be tested.

Overall two-thirds of students enrolled upon Foundation degree programmes in the UK in 2003-04 were female (HESA, 2005b). However, the gender bias in relation to participation is particularly marked when considered on the basis of subject (*see* Table 2 and Figure 5). This is demonstrated through the HESA student data and through the UCAS application and acceptance data.

Subjects (JACS)	Female	Male
Education	97%	3%
Subjects allied to medicine	80%	20%
Social studies	79%	21%
Veterinary science	60%	40%
Business and administrative studies	58%	42%
Creative arts & design	52%	48%
Biological science	42%	58%
Mathematical and computer science	23%	77%
Engineering and technology	9%	91%

Note: 1. Only subject areas with more than 500 students have been included.
2. All percentages have been rounded to the nearest integer.

Table 2: Subject of study by gender
Source: HESA, 2005 (UK)

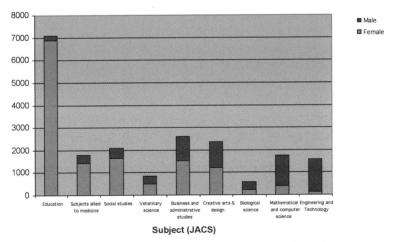

Note: Only subject areas with more than 500 students have been included.

Figure 5: Subject of study by gender
Source: HESA 2005 (UK)

It is worth noting that students enrolled on education programmes (2003-04) were almost exclusively female (97%), and almost half of all female students enrolled on Foundation degree programmes were undertaking Education programmes. Other subject areas in which female students dominated included Subjects allied to medicine (80%), Social studies (79%) and Veterinary science (60%).

Conversely, male students dominated in the subject areas of Engineering and Technology (91%), Mathematical and Computer Science (77%), and Mass Communications and Documentation (68%). Around one-fifth of all male students were enrolled upon programmes in Engineering and Technology.

The HESA data revealed demographic patterns in relation to mode of study. Just under two-thirds (61%) of female students studied on a part-time basis, compared to only a quarter of males (26%). This shows the greater tendency for females to enrol on part-time programmes. The dominance of mature female students on part-time programmes is further illustrated by the fact that in 2003-04, 82% of women enrolled on Foundation degrees were over the age of 21 years (HESA 2005a). However, the classification of part-time and full-time in relation to the mode of study is not as simple as may first appear, as there remains a discontinuity between data categories and actual and perceived modes of delivery (to include flexible, distance and distributed learning modes), which can be further explored through more qualitative approaches.

On the basis of age, around two-fifths of students were aged 25 years and under with the remaining three-fifths 26 years and over (HESA 2005b). This demonstrates that Foundation degree programmes are attracting mature students, though the data reveal a slightly more complex picture than this. Although there was a 50:50 split in terms of mode of study, with half of the students studying part-time and half studying full-time, there were clear variations in mode of study on the basis of age. Around three-quarters of those aged 26 years or over studied on a part-time basis, compared to less than one-fifth of those aged 25 years or under (HESA 2005b). The HESA data additionally shows that around just under one-sixth of all Foundation degree part-time students were aged 25 years or under. This illustrates the tendency for mature students to study on a part-time basis. From this we might infer that the part-time programmes more effectively meet the widening participation agenda than full-time programmes, which provide an opportunity to enter higher education for students from more traditional backgrounds. On the other hand, a more cautious interpretation would be that part-time Foundation degree programmes are at least allowing those in employment to gain a qualification (possibly with an embedded professional qualification) of direct relevance to their employment and supported by their employer.

In the light of the two distinct groups of students enrolled on Foundation degree programmes and the flexible nature of learning patterns, it appears necessary for policy-makers to ensure that the student support infrastructure is adequate to accommodate their differing needs and that admissions systems are suitably robust, flexible and articulated to accommodate the different qualifications and experience that potential students bring.

Clearly, student ethnicity is an additional aspect of the student profile worthy of analysis. The quantitative data available describing all students enrolled on Foundation degree programmes can potentially mask any patterns and trends that may exist in relation to geographical location of provision and/or programme. This is another aspect of participation that is worthy of further investigation through a more localised appraisal of student characteristics.

Highest qualification on entry

Information collected by QAA in support of the survey and review activities provided an overview of the highest qualification on entry of students (see Table 3 and Figure 6). Information is available in respect of around 9,000 student enrolments over the period 2001-02 to 2004-05. The varying qualifications on entry demonstrate the diversity of student backgrounds. The variation in respect of traditional routes of entry is more apparent in respect of part-time students.

Highest qualification on entry	Full-time	Part-time
GCSE	6%	1%
GCE 'A' level/AS level	28%	13%
VCE 'A' level/AS level/Advanced GNVQs	11%	4%
BTEC National Certificate	4%	4%
BTEC National Diploma	15%	7%
Access qualification	6%	9%
NVQ	5%	13%
Other level 3 qualification	10%	19%
Accreditation of Prior Learning	11%	12%
Other (please specify)	4%	18%

Note: All percentages have been rounded to the nearest integer.

Table 3: Breakdown of enrolments by highest qualification on entry
Source: QAA Student Data Tables 2005

Breakdown of enrolments by highest qualification on entry

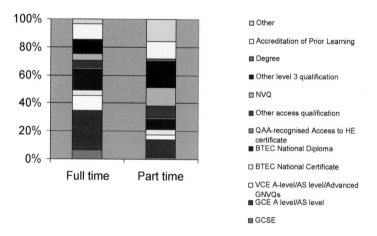

Figure 6: Breakdown of enrolments by highest qualification on entry
Source: QAA Data Tables

These tabulations reveal not only a wide range in respect of the highest qualification in entry, but also that part-time learners and full-time learners tend to enter via different (qualification) routes. It would be interesting to examine whether specific qualification on entry profiles displayed any correlation with programme of study, but such an analysis goes beyond the immediate focus of this chapter.

Almost 40% of full-time students entered their Foundation degree programme with GCE 'A' level/AS levels or VCE 'A' level/AS level/Advanced GNVQs, compared to less than 20% of part-time students. In contrast, part-time learners were significantly more likely to enter the Foundation degree programme with an NVQ or other Level 3 qualifications (32% to 15%), respectively. Around one in 10 full-time and part-time students entered the programme through accreditation of prior (experiential) learning.

In terms of activity prior to enrolment, the data collected to inform the QAA (2004-05) Foundation degree Reviews and surveys reveal that almost all part-time students had been in employment prior to enrolling upon the Foundation degree programme (95%) (see Table 4). Very few part-time students had come directly from education or training. In contrast, the majority of full-time students had enrolled in the programme directly from education or training (54%).

	Full-time	Part-time
Employment	24%	95%
Education/training	54%	1%
Domestic responsibilities	2%	1%
Unemployed and seeking work	3%	1%
Other	4%	0%
Unknown	14%	3%

Note: All percentages have been rounded to the nearest integer.

Table 4: Activity prior to enrolment

Source: QAA Data Tables

The QAA data tables suggest that nearly all part-time students (for whom data are available) continued in employment throughout the programme of study. Just under half of the full-time students continued in relevant employment, and a further quarter in non-related employment. Half of full-time and 3% of part-time students reported no employment during their study.

Over two-thirds of those part-time students who were working reported that they received employer support throughout their programme of study. Although it would be useful to explore the nature of this support in greater detail, its existence in any form suggests the existence of a degree of integration of the academic and vocational skills development as well as of a continued partnership with employers.

Progression, completion and attrition

The QAA data tables reveal that around one-sixth of students enrolled upon Foundation degree courses withdraw from their programme of study (QAA 2005d) and that part-time programmes have a slightly higher withdrawal rate than their full-time counterparts, though it is not possible to ascertain from the data available the general demographic profile of those who withdrew, their reasons for doing so or the point within the programme at which they withdrew. Nonetheless the variability of withdrawal rates from different programmes of study themselves is such as to suggest the desirability of undertaking a systematic comparison of high- and low-withdrawal rate programmes. While around one-third of programmes had a withdrawal rate of over 30%, a small number recorded a rate in excess of 50%.

Due to the relative newness of Foundation degrees, only one-quarter of enrolled students have currently completed (30% of full-time students and 11% of part-time students). Very few students were reported as not continuing due to academic failure (3.5%), indicating that the majority of Foundation degree students continue to be enrolled on programmes of study (QAA 2005d).

Data available through the QAA Reviews (2005d) on post graduation activity cover some 10% of all recorded enrolments. The HESA Destination of Leavers survey will inevitably provide a greater source of information relating to post graduation activity as more cohorts complete. The evidence available shows that a sizeable proportion of students progressed on to articulated awards, but that variation exists on the basis of both programme and mode of study (QAA 2005d). In addition, evidence suggests that those who opted not to articulate, but to return to employment did so either in a new position, or gained a promotion in their current employment. This permits the cautious conclusion that in some circumstances completion of a Foundation degree programme has a variety of positive outcomes for students, and that the Foundation degree qualification is a potentially valuable commodity in the work place, and can provide currency for promotion and improvement of employment prospects (personal and professional development).

Clearly, post graduation activity, with respect to personal and professional enhancement and development in the work place and/or articulation onto an honours degree programme represents a key area of future longitudinal research, which is currently not supported by existing cohort data.

Conclusion

This chapter has presented broad contextual information relating to the provision of, and participation on, Foundation degrees as an intermediate step on the skills ladder and as an encouragement for participation in higher education from non-traditional groups. It has demonstrated that there has been significant expansion in Foundation degrees, in terms of providers, student enrolments and in terms of the diversity of programmes of provision. There is, however, a need to think longer term about future growth in Foundation degrees and how such growth can be best developed and accommodated as a feature of national educational policy.

This chapter demonstrates clear socio-demographic influences on participation in Foundation degrees and confirms the growth in students from non-traditional socio-demographic and academic backgrounds, and the challenges this creates in terms of both admissions and support. It also demonstrates the existence of distinct regional variations in provision, and queries whether this is market led, demand generated or simply reflects the existence of degree-level provision at the awarding institution. It is obvious that the geographical variation in programme availability creates a lack of equivalence in opportunity for potential students, but it is for educational policy-makers to decide whether this is a matter best left to the market or one which requires a guiding hand from government.

This chapter also identifies a striking dualism in terms of gender in particular, and this also creates challenges for providers regarding teaching and learning methods and appropriate student support infrastructures, in order to ensure equitable and appropriate support for all learners. The QAA Foundation degree Reviews found many strengths and good practice in respect of student support and flexibility in modes of delivery and learning. In addition, a correlation was found to exist between retention rates and the student support infrastructure (QAA 2005).

This chapter concludes that Foundation degrees have been successful in widening participation, and also that they have provided a stepping-stone to honours levels programmes – a rather different function. It additionally highlights a number of issues relating to levels of attrition, which are commonly high, but also very variable, for reasons which have yet to be fully understood. High attrition rates more readily emerge at programme level and are somewhat masked by analysis at a broader level. There is a need, however, to consider attrition in relation to qualifications/awards at a similar position in the FHEQ, and consider systems (e.g. support and admissions) in place with regards to progression or activity beyond the Foundation degree programme.

The significant proportion of students undertaking Foundation degree programmes in Education and the additional HEFCE funding allocations for further student places within Education raise questions over the opportunities for progression from Foundation degree programmes on to articulated awards. Questions regarding the opportunities for articulation can be raised in respect of the availability and location of honours degree places. Given the potential limited spatial mobility of many students, progression on to an articulated award is likely to be local, and as such, provision needs to be local, otherwise geography/distance can become a potential barrier.

The growth in Foundation degree students (in absolute numbers and by subject) is not replicated by similar growth and investment in honours degree level programmes. However, in relation to these potential challenges regarding articulation, it is not clear what proportion of students, for example in Education, become teaching assistants or articulate on to a qualified teacher status programme. This uncertainty further suggests the desirability of a longitudinal investigation of the progression and, more ambitiously, subsequent employment patterns of Foundation degree students.

In undertaking research into Foundation degrees and drawing any conclusions, consideration needs to be given to the availability of data and the data sets to be used. The lack of any complete national data set inhibits any holistic UK wide analysis. Additionally problems with research into Foundation degrees are further compounded by the use of different terminology and subject classification structures used by the various data collectors. The lack of a sufficient number of completed cohort data restricts any meaningful longitudinal analysis at this current point in time.

The relative newness of Foundation degree programmes and the untapped information resources that exist present a virgin territory for researchers. However, it is recommended that stakeholders work together on generating research questions to meet national and local agendas. Additionally, there is a need to refine and develop data collection strategies and terminology to ensure that the necessary data are readily available whilst minimising the burden upon providers through avoiding the need for repeated ad hoc data gathering exercises. Combined data collection strategies need to embrace the 'collect once, use many times' philosophy.

There is a wealth of opportunity for investigation and research into Foundation degree programmes to help inform policy-makers, decision-makers and those delivering Foundation degree programmes. The outcomes of research and analysis can provide an information set to help plan for the future, and ensure the equivalence and appropriateness of opportunity for study and progression, and the quality and standards of the learning environment and learning experience.

Note: HESA does not accept responsibility for any inferences or conclusions derived from its data by third parties.

Notes:

[1] QAA Scope and Preference Exercise (QAA 2004) was undertaken in October 2004. HEIs who had awarded Foundation degrees in 2002-03 were requested to provide information regarding programmes currently awarded, student enrolments and sites of delivery. Information was received from over 100 HEIs regarding over 400 programmes.

[2] Data tables from institutions provided information about students enrolled on programmes of study, by delivery site, in support of the surveys and review activities. Data was collected for over 9,000 students enrolled on over 100 programmes of study between 2001-02 to 2004-05 (QAA 2005d).

References

Brown, B.J. (2005) 'Foundation degrees in South West England', *forward,* Issue 6, pp 7-12.

DfES (2003) *The Future of Higher Education.* London: DfES.

fdf (2005) *forward,* Issue 5.

HESA (2005a) PR86. Cheltenham: HESA.

HESA Information Provision Services (2005b) *2003-04 and 2002-03 Student Data.* Unpublished data.

HESA (2005c) *Students in Higher Education Institutions 2003/04, Table 14.* Cheltenham: HESA.

HEFCE (2004) *Foundation degrees: allocation of development funds and additional places.* Bristol: HEFCE 04/15.

Little, B. (2005) 'Policies towards work-focused higher education – are they meeting employers' needs?', *Tertiary Education and Management,* v.11, n.2, pp 131-146.

QAA (2004) *Scope and Preference Survey.* Unpublished data.

QAA (2005a) *Report of a survey to follow up Foundation Degree reviews carried out in 2002-03.* Gloucester: QAA.

QAA (2005b) *Report of a survey of Foundation Degrees converted from existing Higher National Diplomas since 2001.* Gloucester: QAA.

QAA (2005c) *Report of a survey to follow up Foundation Degree reviews carried out in 2002-03.* Gloucester: QAA.

QAA (2005d) *Foundation degree Student data Tables.* Unpublished data

Rowley, J. (2005) 'Foundation degrees: a risky business?', *Quality Assurance in Higher Education,* v.13, n.1, pp 6-16.

UCAS (2005) *2002-2005 Applications Data.* Unpublished data.

Wilson J.P. et al (2005) 'Reconfiguring higher education: the case for Foundation degrees', *Education and Training,* v.47, n.2, pp112-123.

Chapter 4

Recovering the Student Voice:

RETENTION AND ACHIEVEMENT ON FOUNDATION DEGREES

Daphne Hampton and Margo Blythman
London College of Communication
University of the Arts London

Introduction

The first year student experience has a very high profile as a topic in contemporary higher education but how much do we know about what our students really think about their first learning experiences on their Foundation degrees? Recovery of the student 'voice' is an area that Foundation degree practitioners need to consider as part of our strategy to improve the quality of student learning. Our research is located within a form of the interpretivist tradition (for more detail see the later section on 'The research'). Although we would not wish to deny the importance of structural factors in society, we regard knowledge as being constructed through an understanding that different people and groups, in different power relationships, experience the world in different ways. As we argue later, it is important to give 'voice' to the experience of the least powerful.

In this chapter we focus on the student experience, on the highs and lows of the first two terms on some full-time Foundation degrees at the LCC (London College of Communication), a constituent college of the University of the Arts London. Our context is outlined in more detail later in the chapter. We also examine the views of our students on one of our planned strategies to support Foundation degrees: student to student mentoring. Our particular interest is student retention and achievement. As such, the chapter crosses the boundaries of academic research and practical recommendations. Issues that students themselves perceive as creating obstacles to, and opportunities for, student achievement and retention are identified and practical suggestions are made as a result. The student voices inform staff on the action needed to enable research to relate directly to teaching and learning. We locate ourselves as practitioners whose work is underpinned by the scholarship of student support. In this chapter, student support is highlighted as a key component for achieving success, with particular emphasis on the role of student mentors as an aid to engagement and learning. As institutions struggle with increasing student numbers, a more diverse student body and declining resources, a wider range of methods of student support needs to be explored and evaluated and our view is that student mentoring is under-recognised.

Retention and the first year experience

Bousted and May (2003) refer to the crucial role of the first term in retention. There is a growing body of research in the UK on student retention and emerging research suggests that similar findings apply to achievement. Much of the most useful and relevant research, when considering retention of Foundation degree students, comes from further education. It is worth noting that the higher education 'non-traditional' student is the further education 'traditional' student. Further education has been struggling with issues of retention for many more years than higher education and so there is a wealth of experience and literature to be drawn on. Key further education findings suggest that college based initiatives can make a difference, so we should move away from models that individualise student failure and look more to institutional factors (Martinez, 1997). A survey of the literature on further education student retention (Fitzcharles, 2001) concluded that the student experience of the institution is a significant factor in retention and that colleges can adopt strategies which will improve retention rates. Kenwright (1996) found that, even where there was considerable individual difficulty, students persisted if they valued the course enough; if students felt they were having a useful learning experience, they would battle through family problems, health or money difficulties and remain on the course.

The majority of successful strategies identified in the further education literature fall into the following five categories (Blythman and Orr, 2001; 2002):

- best fit initiatives (e.g. through ensuring that the student is on the right course)
- supporting activities (e.g. study support and enrichment activities)
- financial support (e.g. bursaries)
- connective activities which build the connection between the student and the college (e.g. enhanced tutorial and mentoring)
- transformational activities (e.g. raising student expectations and self belief through careers and progression activities).

Evidence also suggests that students who access support have lower drop-out rates (Basic Skills Agency, 1997) and that study support and close monitoring through personal tutorial increases retention of 'at risk' students and improves achievement (Martinez, 2000). Students constantly weigh up the costs and benefits of completion (Martinez and Munday, 1998). It is also important to note that the reasons students give for drop-out depends on who asks the question and there is an argument for ensuring independent research where students feel freer to give their real reasons (Martinez, 1995). It is also important to research those who stay, as well as those who leave, since factors which appear to cause withdrawal, such as financial hardship, may also be true of those who stay (Kenwright, 1996). Overall, factors affecting retention and achievement are likely to be complex, multi-faceted and require a joined-up approach in terms of institutional strategy (Martinez and Munday, 1998).

Turning to higher education, research on retention of undergraduates (e.g. Yorke, 1999) suggests that the following are key factors in causing students to drop out:

- poor quality of student experience
- inability to cope with course demands
- unhappiness with the social environment
- wrong choice of programme
- matters related to financial need
- dissatisfaction with aspects of the course and student support structures.

Research at the London Institute of Education (Coate and Spours, 2003) on retention of part-time MA (Master of Arts) students suggests the following are important institutional factors:

- individual support and formative assessment for students on their first piece of assessed work, particularly written work
- regular, focused and rigorous feedback on assessed work
- 'early course practices' such as interviewing potential students and thorough induction into course and course expectations
- recognition that requests to defer on assessments may indicate the student is at risk.

Of course, the students in the Coate and Spours study were experienced learners who were educational professionals but it is interesting to note that, if these factors were important for relatively sophisticated learners, how much more important they might be for Foundation degree students. Yorke and Thomas (2003) highlight the importance of early formative assessment and within this of the pre-entry and first year experience in particular. Johnstone (1997) points out that early identification of at risk students is essential for their retention and achievement. However, it is not always easy to bring about supportive changes in the way courses are delivered. Taylor and Bedford (2004) suggest that, within retention discussions, academic staff tend to focus on student-based factors rather than issues of teaching and learning methodology and the curriculum.

The first year student experience is a current priority across the UK. Of particular interest is the work of the Scottish higher education 'Enhancement Themes' (www.enhancementthemes.ac.uk). This work is coordinated by the Scottish Higher Education Enhancement Committee, made up of all the main bodies in Scotland that have a stake in quality enhancement within higher education. This approach has much to offer those of us working outside Scotland. It is addressing the fundamental question 'what do we really want students to get out of their first year?' The committee's first enhancement theme is the first year curriculum, with a focus on structure, content and "the extent to which the co-curriculum can be owned by the students themselves". Its second enhancement theme is empowerment:

> "… to equip them at the start of their studies with the skills, capacities and knowledge to be as effective as possible as independent learners for the rest of their programme, and for their subsequent employability, professional development, and for that matter, lifelong learning". (QAA Scotland, 2003: p2)

This theme includes, as a key idea, trying as far as possible to tailor the provision to the individual by providing considerable feedback and help on progress at this individual level. The second key idea highlighted by this enhancement theme is to re-examine the whole nature of induction and see it as a process over a period of time rather than a series of one-off events.

The third enhancement theme, which the authors acknowledge is the most challenging, is that of student engagement. They argue that:

> "… this sub-theme should primarily focus on the learners' relationship with peers: how can an institutional culture acknowledge and help to shape the attitudes and norms that are so influential in the first year experience? Ideas that will be explored might include peer-mentoring, peer-support and peer-tutoring of first-year students by students from later in their programmes; collaborative work that is carefully designed and carefully led to encourage the nurturing of peer-relationships

that engage with learning tasks; establishing a culture of sharing learning outputs (especially through emerging technology); and encouraging engagement with employability issues in the first year curriculum". (QAA Scotland, 2003: pp.2-3)

Of particular interest in this last theme is a recognition that higher education is under pressure in relation to resources and student numbers and there is a need to move more of the responsibility for learning to the students. But this is approached through a serious attempt to identify authentic enhancing experiences rather than pat 'solutions' which satisfy the finance director but not the students.

At LCC we wish to engage with these issues and argue that a starting point is students' perception of the current experience. Many students have compelling stories to tell and listening to the student voice about the first term is important. It can help staff reflect on what is required in order to offer the learning experience that students need to encourage them to stay on and fulfil their potential on their Foundation degree.

Our research is related to a student support model which sees 'student failure' as a complex concept requiring considerable critical examination including a focus on how this is experienced by the student (Peelo et al, 2002). This research into recovering the student voice can help staff change their views on what retention means and how best to achieve it.

LCC and Foundation degrees

LCC has been delivering Foundation degrees since 2001-02 and offers them in a range of subjects within the specialist Art, Design and Communication curriculum. At the time of writing, in 2006, LCC has 15 Foundation degrees with almost 1,000 students. All these courses are full-time and attract both those new to higher education and some who wish to convert from other disciplines as a form of career change. These include such areas as Interior Design, Media Practice, Journalism and Surface Design. The University of the

Arts London has its own further education offering and tries to ensure progression routes right through from further education to research degree. For this reason, perhaps unusually, all our Foundation degrees are fully taught within the university rather than local colleges. For those students who wish, and are able, to continue beyond Foundation degrees to BA (Bachelor of Arts, honours), there is no need to change institution and indeed LCC is now developing some 'top-up' years to tailor this opportunity better for graduates of Foundation degrees.

LCC is strongly committed to personal academic tutorials and study support (Jackson and Blythman, forthcoming) as key aspects of its strategies for high student retention and achievement within the context of widening participation. Student to student mentoring is another key strand in the overall student support policy. It is as committed to changing university structures and cultures as it is to 'adjusting' the individual student to cope with existing practices (Jackson and Blythman, forthcoming).

The research

Listening to and acting on the student voice means staff can encourage the institution to organise its support activities around the needs of the students (HEFCE, 2003: p.17). On a more conceptual level, we believe that people experience the world in different ways, largely affected by their power position in particular contexts. The social world is understood through a variety of perspectives coming from multiple realities and this is best captured through social actors being able to "name the world" (Freire 1996: p.69). Our methodology for this is semi-structured interviews. For these reasons we report our research following with an emphasis on the students' own words.

The research explored how the students perceive barriers to learning in their first two terms at LCC by the use of semi-structured interviews with 15 students across three full-time Foundation degree courses, in Interior Design, Travel and Tourism, and Visual Design and Display. We chose these courses because we wanted to focus on the experience within one School in case there were School specific factors. Our research interest was to focus on the high points and low points of their perception of their experiences in an open way that did not prejudge what issues would be important to them as opposed to the standard student feedback questionnaire. Our student sample was quite mature, almost half were over 30 and more than half of our respondents came from outside the UK, mainly other EU countries. The interviews explored aspects of the students' lives before and during terms one and two with a focus on what, in their eyes, had been good or bad experiences.

Research findings

The first notable finding was that most students were using the course to help with a career change.

> When I left school, I think I took the wrong career path. I was more or less persuaded not to go to art college because my parents asked 'what are you going to do at the end of it?'...I've always regretted not having done something creative. I'm at a time in my life when my son is older and luckily I can afford to take time off to do this course.
>
> (Julie - female, 46 years old)

> I wanted a new break as my husband passed away and I had always been creative at home. One day I was reading at home and I saw the advert (for the Foundation degree course)"
>
> (Soraya - female, 54 years old)

> Well, I did a City and Guilds course, but on reflection I really wish I'd come to the Access course here before doing this Foundation degree....It would have given me a good stepping stone into this course, which I am doing to change career direction.
>
> (Emma - female, 39 years old)

This would suggest that Foundation degrees are making a contribution to the employability agenda as well as widening participation.

Students were asked to describe their experience of the first term. Eight main themes emerged.

The first was the pressure that students felt combining home and work commitments with studying, a finding one might expect with a group including a number of mature students.

> *Well, I have a family as well and I need to spend some time with them so it's quite hard to fit everything in....college, work and family you know.*
>
> (Soraya)

Secondly, they reported strong feelings of being overwhelmed by so many new experiences.

> *Well, initially I found it all overwhelming. It was all new and you're not quite sure what you are doing. Sometimes you're given a talk on something or you're given a brief and you don't always know what the tutor wants. You're doing your best but you're not always sure whether what you're doing is correct, but it seems to come right in the end.*
>
> (Julie)

However, this was ameliorated by their perception of good student support being available.

> *I like the course because I have a fantastic tutor....he's very nice and makes you feel good when you are coming to the course, which stops you worrying about all the new things. The tutor is very special and he really likes what he does here.*
>
> (Michelle - female, 24 years old)

Thirdly, the students stressed how enjoyable the course was, with good information and good staff.

> *It's been just fine. I didn't expect it to be as hard, because there's a lot of work to be done. I really like it though, it's enjoyable.*
>
> (Lucy - female, 18 years old)

> *I enjoy the course. The staff are great. I enjoy coming to college every day and learning new stuff.*
>
> (Miguel - male, 20 years old)

Fourthly, students showed appreciation of the practical nature of the course, especially compared to an honours degree taken previously by one of the respondents. She was studying the Foundation degree within a few years of graduating and was using the Foundation degree to change career direction.

> *It is much more practical and useful than the honours degree.*
>
> (Adeye - female, 28 years old)

> *When I came for the interview, the building was full of end-of-year shows and it was quite an inspiration. There was some beautiful work on display and it's always had a really high reputation. So when I was accepted onto the course I was really pleased that I would be doing work like that.*
>
> (Julie)

The other four key findings that emerged from the analysis of the student interviews were more critical of the experience but in terms of general criticisms that students, on all kinds of courses and institutions, make of contemporary UK higher education. They reported that they felt the classes were too big and daunting, the problems of being a foreigner with no family in the UK making it harder to study, the lack of enough high quality equipment and the pressures of group work.

> *It's been quite good because the course is good and the people here are really good as well. It's just the group work is a bit pressuring.*
>
> (Lucy)

The students were then asked what their best experience was in the first term. Seven aspects were reported, with many respondents combining two or more.

The seven were:
- doing well in the first project/getting 'A' grades in the first term
- all the support to help integrate into the course and college
- learning new things
- meeting new people
- gaining confidence
- knowledgeable and enthusiastic lecturers
- learning practical knowledge and skills in a specialist area.

The following quotations illustrate these points:

> *The best thing would be meeting new people, and obviously learning new stuff.*
>
> (Miguel)

> *Well, we were offered quite a lot of support, which I found fantastic. I was worried to start with as I am a mature student but I found an incredible response from everyone.*
>
> (Soraya)

> *Getting A grades, that was fantastic. I had never got A grades at school.*
>
> (Emma)

> *Well, basically I've really enjoyed absorbing all the information really. And meeting new friends and getting more confident in my drawing skills again and now I'm a little more confident in my own abilities.*
>
> (Julie)

Bousted and May (2004) argue that networks and friendships are a main source of academic and personal support which can start with the induction programme. A welcoming atmosphere from the group, the lecturers and the institution is seen as important. We argue that the most important thing to plan for student induction is the kind of atmosphere you want to create.

Activities that enable students to get to know each other, as well as the teaching team, are vital. Students on these Foundation degrees tell us that meeting new people, gaining confidence and all the support to help integrate into the course and college were some of their best experiences in term one.

Students were also asked, as part of the research, about their worst experience of their first term. Four students reported that they had not had a worst experience.

> *I don't think there is a worst thing for me. I'm finding it all quite positive. I mean some days you get a bad day where things don't always go quite as well as you'd like, but, no, I'm finding that I enjoy it all.*
>
> (Julie)

For other students balancing college, home and work emerged as their worst experience.

> *Even though I found that the course probably wasn't quite as intense as I imagined it to be, I think that balancing the college work and home is enough of a struggle for me....it has meant that I have less time for things outside college.*
>
> (Emma)

Yorke's (2000) findings regarding factors affecting student decisions to leave include the inability to cope with course demands, together with matters related to financial need. Balancing college, home and work could include both these factors.

Four students stated that the realisation that their IT skills were very limited was their worst experience. Universities are sometimes deceived by the sophistication of the IT skills of younger students and forget that there is still a backlog of students whose education may pre-date the digital age. HEFCE (2003) cites educational background as a factor affecting retention and this includes exposure to IT skills.

One student reported time management problems as her worst experience, stating that this was more complicated than balancing college, home and work. This student wanted guidance on prioritising college assignments, reading, lectures and seminars/studio work as well as help with balancing the college, home, work portfolio.

> *Handing my essays and other assignments in on time, meeting the deadlines, was my worst experience. I didn't know which one to do first and then there were all the lectures and briefs to do and I didn't know if I was allowed to miss anything... and I work part-time and want to meet my friends and see my family.*
>
> (Lucy)

Two students referred to the college learning environment, specifically the poor heating, as their worst experience. Sometimes we forget or under estimate the importance of these environmental factors but listening to students often reminds us of how grim it can be to work in a building that is always too hot or too cold, or with inadequate lifts or other infrastructure problems.

The potential of student mentoring schemes

We also wanted to investigate students' views on the potential usefulness of having student to student mentoring systems and to investigate the student experience of mentoring. Yorke and Thomas (2003) emphasise the importance of a supportive, friendly first year climate and point out that students' patterns of engagement with universities is changing and we need to recognise this. Topping (1996, quoted in Falchicov, 2001) defines mentoring as "a 1:1 supportive relationship between the student and another person of greater ability or experience".

LCC has had small scale mentoring schemes on honours degree courses for several years and found them to be beneficial. Mentoring helps students settle into the course and college culture while enabling them to fulfil their academic potential, with consequent good retention. With widening participation on institutional agendas, mentoring schemes provide an additional tool in the armoury of support for at risk students. We wanted to discover Foundation degree students' views on mentoring, in particular potential benefits of such schemes and the qualities needed by a mentor. We were interested in how Foundation degree students thought they would benefit if they had the help of a second year student. Also we needed to know what they would like help with. Again, research into the student voice leads to practical recommendations.

The students were asked if they had ever heard of student mentoring schemes. Most students had but none had participated in one. Before engaging with this aspect of the interviews, the students were given a brief description of the role of a mentor and were then asked what qualities they thought were needed to be a good mentor. The following factors emerged:

- good knowledge of the course and college
- being approachable
- good listening skills
- being motivating
- patience
- honesty and trustworthiness
- being hardworking
- helpfulness
- friendliness
- having time for the *student being mentored* - as a person
- being encouraging
- intelligence.

Almost all students thought it would make no difference whether a student mentor was male or female. One student disagreed.

> *I think females might give other females more time but males would be more objective in their help.*
>
> (Emma)

All 15 respondents stated that the mentor's personality would be the most important factor for them. On being asked why it would be good to have a student mentor in year one, the students gave the following replies.

First, to learn techniques and skills:

> *Well, they can help them. If the second year's done the same thing as the first year's done, it'll help the first year see what to do. Give them ideas and learning new skills and how to do their work.*
>
> (Lucy)

Second, to get support/advice with assignments and with college life:

> *If I had a mentor here, I'd be able to sort of ring him or her and say 'have you got a minute?'...and 'could you go through that with me?'...and (discuss) how they'd managed themselves through the course.*
>
> (Emma)

Third, to brainstorm problems:

> *...well, discuss basic ideas and what you need to do in your assignments.*
>
> (Melissa - 21 years old)

Fourth, to help improve/see what is possible:

> *I think we'd have lots of questions how you go about things....what I'm doing, can I do it better, can I improve? I think the second year students know much more than the first years. It would be great, actually. I would gain more motivation and more determination.*
>
> (Soraya)

> *I think really if I had any problems, and maybe had some doubts in my own ability, maybe the mentor would say 'look don't worry about that because I had the same problem but I've overcome it by some extra courses' or 'I've had a chat to somebody that's given me a little bit of extra help' and I think that can be quite positive to think that other people have had the same problems and they've managed to overcome them.*
>
> (Soraya)

Fifth, to give guidance:

> *I feel that they could steer us in the right direction, more than the tutors, in which way to handle assignments. And I think that would be a great advantage, especially for someone like me because sometimes I will read the brief and it goes over the top of my head.*
>
> (Alice - female, 35 years old)

Sixth, to learn about the course:

> *They would tell us about the course itself and what you should achieve, what things you'll be learning and stuff like that, and what you should work for.*
>
> (Lucy)

> *Well, I'd probably be ready for the following year and know what to expect.*
>
> (Miguel)

Clearly, mentoring is seen as promoting an awareness of the norms, values and practices of the academic world. It can improve confidence and increase subject knowledge. Owen (2002) states that a good induction programme is essential but may produce an overload of information which will be forgotten within three months. These Foundation degree students perceive mentors as a way of keeping this knowledge alive and fresh in their minds. Mentors can act as a form of 'ongoing induction' (Bousted and May, 2003). They can also provide informal feedback to complement the formal feedback of assessment, enabling students to learn more from each experience. But they also have another role for the university. New students are likely to talk more freely, and have more opportunity for individual informal conversations with mentors, which can then be fed back, anonymised, to the course and university to help identify issues of concern to students and what they regard particularly positively. So mentoring in itself becomes another channel for the student voice.

The need for more research

Having conducted this small scale research project our view is that we need to know much more about how Foundation degree students experience higher education. Listening to the student voice should be one way of achieving this all important goal. More research that recovers the student voice should be undertaken within Foundation degrees to help achieve this. Analysis of the overall findings reveals some interesting discussion points and areas for further research. Many of the students interviewed were using their Foundation degree to help with a career change. Are many of our students studying Foundation degrees in order to facilitate a career change? Is this the experience across the country? If so, there are interesting policy implications which would also benefit from research. It might make us re-consider the way we introduce the employability agenda into the courses. Another key research area is those students who do not complete successfully. We chose to focus on those who stayed because so much recent focus has been on those who drop out but we do need research which listens to those for whom Foundation degrees did not work. Again, some longitudinal studies to examine the student experience over the duration of the course would enable us to have more than brief snapshots and we would hope that, as the number of Foundation degree students increases and graduates, there will be studies of their progression beyond Foundation degrees into both top-up years and employment.

The way forward

Our respondents' accounts of the best experience of the first term show students valuing opportunities to gain confidence and meet new people. The student voice also tells us the importance of strong student support to help integrate into the course and college. These aspects should be built on and reinforced by Foundation degree course teams in pre-entry, induction and the first term. For our respondents this support is one of the most positive factors in their learning journey. The student voice also tells us that learning new and practical knowledge and skills in a specialist area is one of their best experiences in term one, reminding us that "the nature of success for the learner is measured against the usefulness of the qualification and of the skills and knowledge gained" (Calder,1993).

Looking at worst experiences reported, the realisation of their very limited IT skills was identified by four respondents. This may reflect the numbers of mature students on the courses and shows that institutions should not take IT skills for granted, but offer diagnostic sessions, followed by confidence boosting IT training sessions. Balancing college, home and work was also reported as the worst experience by four students: this highlights the necessity of strong student support being offered to help students with these issues in term one.

On the basis of our findings we would wish to argue the following. The provision of student mentors is seen as very helpful by all our respondents. Serious thought should be given to providing a student mentoring scheme on the first year of Foundation degree programmes. Additionally, an excellent support infrastructure in the first term is essential. This should be there for the whole year and not just induction. Good support must also be offered at the pre-entry stage. Student mentors play a key role in reminding their *charges* of what support is available, the ongoing induction (Bousted and May, 2003), which recognises the need to treat induction as a process, not an event.

Foundation degree first year students need to feel that they are being taught by enthusiastic, knowledgeable and caring staff. The student voice shows that they see this as a key factor in their success. Managers should pick with care those teaching and managing first year Foundation degree courses. Of course this is not without its problems. We would argue that within the current pressurised environment in higher education, research continues to have more status than teaching and that even within teaching any kind of student nurturing activity has even less status in a way which can be perceived as gendered. Morley (1998) points out that the 'emotional labour' of offering support and being caring often falls to women.

We argue, however, that students value the practical specialist skills available from studying a Foundation degree and they tell us that they need their confidence building from the very start. This includes pre-entry as well as induction. Extra resources devoted to the first term bring the student good benefits and are valued by them, and are likely to contribute to improvements in retention and achievement.

Additionally, large classes are seen as very daunting. Many Foundation degree students are mature returnees or have come from Access or similar courses and are unused to such learning environments. Thought must be given to making these large group learning experiences a more human proposition for the student. The use of sub-groups within groups and even sub-sub groups, ensuring that all students have a structured very small group to which they belong, can make a contribution to a student sense of community. Finally, some mature students are arriving with limited IT skills and plans must be in place to identify these students early and give them the skills they require while not undermining their confidence further.

Finally, Foundation degrees have enormous potential for British higher education. They make an important contribution to widening participation and the employability agenda and are therefore of both social and economic importance. There are many ways of evaluating their impact on the UK higher education system and our view is that, as part of this evaluation, we have a responsibility to understand as many dimensions of them as possible through the students' accounts of their experience. Foundation degrees have the opportunity to offer students a unique and valued experience but we as practitioners have to continue to work to ensure this potential.

Bibliography

Basic Skills Agency (1997) *Staying the Course.* London: Basic Skills Agency.

Blythman, M. and Orr, S. (2001) 'Joined up policy: a strategic approach to improving retention in the UK', *Journal of College Retention Studies,* v. 3, n.3.

Blythman, M. and Orr, S. (2002) 'Learning from FE: a joined up approach to student support', in M. Peelo & T. Wareham (eds.), *Failing Students in Higher Education.* Buckingham: Society for Research into Higher Education (SRHE)/Open University.

Bousted, M. and May, S. (2003) 'Shall I stay or shall I go: students who leave Kingston University in semester one', *Educational Developments,* 4.2.

Calder, J (1993) *Disaffection and Diversity - overcoming barriers for adult learners.* London: The Falmer Press.

Coate, K. and Spours, K. (2003) 'Student survey on successful completion; implications for policy and practice'. Paper delivered at Institute of Education conference *Teaching and Learning in Higher Education,* April 2003.

Falchicov, N. (2001) *Learning Together: peer tutoring in higher education.* London: RoutledgeFalmer.

Fitzcharles, N. (2001) 'A report on factors influencing the retention of students in further education', in Scottish Further Education Unit (ed.) *Policy and Practice: Studies in Further Education Vol. 3.* Edinburgh: SFEU.

Freire, P. (1996) *Pedagogy of the Oppressed.* London: Penguin.

HEFCE (2003) *Supporting Higher Education in Further Education Colleges: a guide for tutors and lecturers.* Bristol: HEFCE.

Jackson, S. and Blythman, M. (forthcoming) 'Just coming through the door was hard: supporting students with mental health difficulties', in Babcocket, R.D. et al (eds.) *Writing Centers and Disability.* Illinois: Southern Illinois University Press.

Johnstone, V. (1997) 'Why do first year students fail to progress to their second year? An academic staff perspective'. Paper presented at *BERA Annual Conference,* University of York, 11-14 Sept. 1997.

Kenwright, H. (1996) *Developing Retention Strategies: did they fall or were they pushed?* York: York College of Further and Higher Education.

Martinez, P. (1995) *Student Retention in Further and Adult Education: the evidence.* Blagdon: FEDA.

Martinez, P. (1997) *Improving Student Retention: a guide to successful strategies.* Blagdon: FEDA.

Martinez, P. (2000) *Raising Achievement: a guide to successful strategies.* Blagdon: FEDA

Martinez, P. and Munday, F. (1998) *9000 Voices: student persistence and drop-out in further education.* Blagdon: FEDA.

Morley, L. (1998) 'All you need is love: feminist pedagogy for empowerment and emotional labour in the academy', *International Journal of Inclusive Education,* v.2, n.1, pp.15-27.

Owen, M. (2002) 'Sometimes you feel you're in niche time: the personal tutor system, a case study', *Active Learning in Higher Education,* v. 3, n.1.

Peelo, M. and Wareham, T.F. (2002) 'Who is failing - defining student failure?' in Peelo, M. and Wareham, T.F. (eds.) *Failing Students in Higher Education.* Buckingham: SRHE/Open University Press.

QAA Scotland (2003) *Enhancement themes: 'the first year' - proposed approach.* Document available from http://www.enhancementthemes.ac.uk/. Last accessed: 29 June 2006.

Scottish Enhancement Themes (2006) www.enhancementthemes.ac.uk. Last accessed: 29 June 2006.

Taylor, J. A. and Bedford, T. (2004) 'Staff perceptions of factors related to non-completion in higher education', *Studies in Higher Education,* v.29, n.3: pp.375-394.

Thomas, L. (2002) 'Building social capital to improve student success'. Paper given at *BERA Conference,* University of Exeter, September 2003.

Topping, K.J. (1996) 'Effective peer tutoring in further and higher education'. SEDA Paper 95. Birmingham: Staff and Educational Development Association.

Yorke, M. (1999) *Leaving Early: undergraduate non-completion in higher education.* London: Falmer Press.

Yorke, M. (2000) 'The quality of student experience: what can students learn from data relating to non–completion?', *Quality in Higher Education,* v.6, n.1.

Yorke, M. and Thomas, L. (2003) 'Improving the retention of students from lower socio-economic groups', *Journal of Higher Education Policy and Management,* v.25, n.1: pp. 63-74.

3

Aspects of Practice: assessment, curriculum development and work based learning

Chapter 5

Foundation Degree Assessment Models

MEETING THE NEEDS OF THE
NEW GENERATION OF HIGHER LEVEL
STUDENTS ON HOSPITALITY
MANAGEMENT FOUNDATION DEGREES

Conor Sheehan
Westminster Kingsway College

Introduction

The most significant curriculum initiative of the last five years has been the introduction of Foundation degrees, which were launched in February 2000. The Dearing Report (1997) concluded that graduates should benefit from increased "work readiness" and that there was a need for greater collaboration and harmonization between industry and higher education sectors. There has since been a growing imperative for curriculum design in higher education in order to incorporate this vision of vocationally contextualized learning. In 2000, David Blunkett, then Secretary of State for

Education, explained the rationale for the introduction of Foundation degrees thus:

> "Foundation Degrees will raise the value of vocational and technical qualifications making them an attractive first choice for many students. A two year route to a degree with high market value because of its focus on employability will offer a new option for people, both young and mature, who do not feel that a traditional, three year honours degree is right for them." (DfEE, 2000)

Following this, the 2003 government White Paper on the *Future of Higher Education* (DfES, 2003) made it clear that Foundation degrees were central to the government's strategy for aligning vocational education at higher education level with the needs of the 'new generation' student and of increasing participation. Foundation degree programmes were to be different in terms of their approach to delivery, curriculum content and emphasis on work-related learning.

New forms of learning, by implication, require new forms of assessment. The research reported on here was concerned with investigating the need, at institutional and industry levels, to review existing assessment strategies. It focused on the challenges of developing more vocationally relevant forms of assessment whilst simultaneously preserving academic rigor. Such developments presented a challenge to learning providers and industry professionals alike as there was now a need for them to work closely together. The research study involved a review of contemporary literature on issues such as curriculum and assessment design, student support, mentoring and e-tutoring.

One of the key requirements for Foundation degrees is that they be designed in collaboration with employers from the vocational sector to which they relate.[1] It is intended that Foundation degree programmes combine a mix of work-related specialist skills development with academic learning. It is also important that they are capable of being studied in a variety of locations -

including traditional in-college attendance, the workplace and home – as well as virtually, using on-line technology. By implication, the qualification not only encourages more innovative ways of teaching and learning but also requires more innovative and alternative methods of assessment to support their delivery. Many colleges and universities have been challenged to develop methods of assessment that incorporate both the need for flexibility and direct vocational relevance. This chapter documents a research project which investigated potential approaches to Foundation degree assessment on Hospitality Management programmes.[2] The study relates specifically to work conducted on the design and implementation of assessment within the School of Hospitality, Leisure and Tourism at Westminster Kingsway College, London. The focus was on the development of two particular aspects of assessment: (1) a suitable model or models for possible collaborative activity between students and between students, module/course teams and employers, and (2) appropriate modes of communication between assessor, student and employer. The central aim of the research was to recommend a model of assessment design with specific relevance to Hospitality Management Foundation degrees but also with more universal applicability to programmes in other vocational areas.[3]

Research methods and data sources

The study involved a review of contemporary research literature on issues such as curriculum and assessment design, student support, mentoring and e-tutoring. Qualitative field research methods were used to explore existing good practice in assessment design and delivery and the perceptions of academic practitioners involved in the delivery of this new programme. The primary research also investigated the views and expressed needs of two other key stakeholder groups: Foundation degree students and hospitality sector employers. The initial primary and secondary research and writing up took place over an eight-week period from March to May 2003 but a follow-up study was conducted in 2004 as part of an investigation into a wider range of issues relating to Foundation degree delivery models. The literature search investigated some current views on higher education assessment and how these perceptions might apply to Foundation degrees and the sections that follow summarize the key themes that emerged.

Contemporary views on assessment design

Rust (2002) suggests that there has been a worldwide paradigm shift towards student-centred outcome-based approaches in vocational education. He implies that assessment can no longer be viewed as a primarily summative activity, which merely tests and records students' knowledge, skills or abilities but should be viewed as an integral part of the total student experience, where it has a key role in defining the curriculum and the nature of the learning experience. Brown (1997) adds to this that assessment broadly defines what students see as important and what they give priority to. The important implication that he draws is that if we want to influence student learning then we need to change the method of assessment. This view has particular relevance to Foundation degree programmes which have embedded at the heart of their philosophy the notion of innovative and flexible teaching and learning practices. By implication, the assessment models developed by Foundation degree course teams must complement the learning and teaching strategy and provide the same levels of flexibility and innovation as the rest of the student experience.

Buswell (2003) highlights recurring deficiencies in assessment identified by the *QAA* in its 2003 Review of Foundation degrees (QAA, 2003). A consistent and common weakness related to the relationship between learning outcomes, assessment criteria, marking and the written feedback provided for students. 'Outcome-based' approaches to learning are not, however, without their critics. A number of authors have pointed to significant obstacles to introducing and implementing outcomes based approaches, the most significant of which relate to cultural change and the reconceptualisation of what we regard as learning. Jones (2004) further develops the debate with respect to hospitality management education and suggests that it is not only teaching but also hospitality research that has suffered because of the current preoccupation with outcomes and direct vocational relevance. However, the QAA and other agencies articulate clearly the need for Foundation degree programmes that develop students' specific skills and capabilities within a vocational discipline. They emphasize particularly the importance of what graduates actually do and where they progress with the knowledge and abilities acquired in the course of their learning.

Approaches to vocationally contextualized assessment

There is substantial literature relating to the benefits and practice of work based learning and support for students at both further and higher education levels (Fagenson 1989; Clutterbruck 1991; Carruthers 1993; Burke et al, 1994; Orpen 1997; Dutton et al, 2001; McGugan 2003). Moore (2001) and her research collaborators at the University of Warwick's Centre for Education and Industry carried out extensive work on the development of good practice guidelines in work-related teaching and learning. While much of this project focused on post compulsory education, the findings have, arguably, considerable application and relevance to higher education students as well. Moore proposes that employers can benefit students greatly by participating in support programmes and that their contributions could include, for example, providing curriculum advice, mentoring, supervising work-based projects, delivering guest lectures, and providing work experience opportunities. Dutton et al (2001) endorse this view whilst also emphasizing the distinctive benefits for the 'mentor organization'. The advantages they suggest include the generation of 'purpose in their job' for mentors, the opportunity for viewing alternative perspectives, the chance for professional reflection, potential recruitment opportunities and lower associated costs.

For over a decade, Hospitality Management programmes at several universities have involved a significant element of employer contributions to assessment. Lockwood (2002) describes how the use of live casework can be successfully linked to assessment and he documents an assessment project involving key hospitality employers and final year honours degree students. Students had to work in groups to come up with solutions to three significant problems facing the companies. The employers then assessed their proposals. Lockwood asserts that there are many benefits associated with such forms of vocationally contextualised assessment, including the fostering of students' creativity and the generation of useful ideas for industry practitioners. However he cautions that this method of assessment is extremely time consuming, both for academic staff and industry colleagues. A later section of this chapter revisits this theme of employer participation in the light of more recent reports on collaborative assessment approaches.

Computer mediated learning and assessment

The imperative for more flexible delivery of Foundation degree programmes has led to the consideration of alternative approaches which embrace the new teaching, learning and assessment technologies. Two key objectives of the research study were, therefore, to (1) identify an appropriate role for VLEs (Virtual Learning Environments) in Foundation degree assessment, and (2) examine how VLEs could support students during preparation for assessment and the assessment process itself. There is substantial research literature on the application of electronic conferencing to student learning, e-moderating skills and good practice in the design of on-line learning activities (from a large body of literature see, for example, Salmon, 2004 and Parchoma, 2005; and the endnote for a more complete listing)[4]. There has also been considerable work done on the development of on-line assessment programmes. However the literature focusing specifically on this aspect is somewhat smaller (Cann and Pawley, 1999; Salmon, 2002; Rust, 2002), particularly with regard to assessment of hospitality students at higher education level (McGugan, 2001, 2003).

There appears to be a general consensus amongst practitioners and researchers that there are significant learning benefits inherent in the use of VLEs as an aid to assessment. Phillips et al (2000) identify the specific learning benefits of VLEs in terms, for example, of the removal of geographical limits, the potential for less conventional modes of attendance, more flexible patterns of study, greater time for reflection, easier dissemination of learning materials, and greater access to expert help. Phillips et al and Salmon (2002), however, identify the limitations of VLEs, in relation, for example, to problems of accessibility for non traditional learners, the potential cost to the student, the lack of social cues in an on-line environment and the possibility of information overload.

Salmon (2002) asserts that the use of CMC (Computer Mediated Communication) for learning reflects the broadening acceptance and understanding of learning as a socially constructed process. She claims that many institutions offer assessment models which are still based on the 'transmission model of learning'. The concern here is that there may be a widening gap between how students learn and how they are assessed. These observations raise questions about the media within which we assess and how the concept of knowledge and its construction is changing as a direct result of new forms of communication. Such changes need to be reflected in the new assessment models developed for 'new generation' courses such as the Foundation degree. Salmon implies that practitioners need not just reflect on *how* they assess (i.e. the chosen vehicle and medium) but *what* they assess (i.e. the type of knowledge). Buswell's (2003) arguments for "constructive alignment" in the design of assessment have significance here as they ask academic practitioners to question closely how coherently the given learning outcomes are linked to the assessment criteria. As Salmon suggests, conventional assessment criteria are frequently designed around the transmission model of learning and are therefore no longer suitable for new forms of VLE based assessment.

The research findings

At the time of the initial research (April 2003), there were approximately 26 Foundation degrees nationally in Hospitality or Hospitality related areas being offered within university/college consortia.

Early in the enquiry, it became evident that the number of consortia listed as offering Hospitality Foundation degrees considerably outnumbered the consortia actually *delivering* them (there were approximately nine that did). Many providers (i.e. either universities or further education colleges) had not recruited and some colleges had actually deferred the validation process with the intention of offering Foundation degrees from 2005 onwards. This pattern has persisted with the number of institutions offering Foundation degrees in Hospitality increasing but with some providers continuing to report low recruitment numbers and some closing their courses. In research terms it was necessary therefore to adopt a more contingent research strategy which focused on institutions offering more broadly related Foundation degree programmes such as Travel, Tourism, Leisure and Sport Science.

Hospitality practitioner views on employer participation in learning and assessment

One of the starting points for the study was the idea that industry involvement in the design and delivery of teaching and assessment on the new Foundation degree programmes would be key. This view was taken in the light of the rationale underpinning Foundation degrees to forge new links between employers, universities and colleges and to fuse academic and vocational routes to higher-level education. Early in the primary research process, it became evident that the extent and nature of industry participation needed to be reconsidered. To date, some hospitality employers have generously contributed to the overall course development of new Foundation degrees but their feedback indicates that they are uninterested in taking formal responsibility for assessment. All nine hospitality or health related exercise course teams interviewed explained these employers' views similarly: collaborative assessment involving employers would simply be 'too complicated'. One education practitioner expressed her reservations thus:

> *HE Quality Systems are difficult enough for us to get our own heads around; trying to get the employers on board with assessment would be simply mind-blowing! They would be bound to feel vulnerable about taking responsibility within an assessment system that could expose their shortcomings and have them fall flat on their face.*

It was indicated by most practitioners surveyed (seven) within the higher education/further education sectors that employer involvement in course development and delivery should be confined to areas where they felt comfortable and could make a meaningful contribution. These areas included: consultation on module content and programme structure, involvement in the initial design phase, and the provision of work placements. Some education sector respondents suggested that employers, if willing, were better placed to assess aspects of students' key skills during work placement and could do so provided an uncomplicated system of record keeping was introduced. Most institutional respondents emphasized the need to find ways of developing positive relationships with the vocational sectors which were relevant to the qualifications offered. The quality, nature and extent of employer involvement were held to be closely correlated with such relationships. Cotterill (2002) supports this view and shows how such good relations influence students' work-based learning during industrial placement. He also emphasizes how the work environment offers a range of excellent assessment opportunities provided the student brief is well designed and that the management of the assessment process rests primarily with the educational institution. Rogers (2001) and Dutton et al (2001) suggest that 'appropriate' employer involvement in learning and assessment may relate more to 'mentoring' and 'coaching' and that in such roles they have a real opportunity to contribute to the student's development. This view corroborates other opinions from education sector practitioners that mentoring support may be more appropriate for employers than direct involvement in the formal assessment process.

Whilst many learning providers reported the existence of positive and fruitful employer-education collaboration, many also commented on the difficulties of incorporating mentoring and work-based assessment activities into degree programmes. The chief obstacles to formalizing such employer involvement arrangements related usually to the demanding work patterns and shortage of time characteristic of the hospitality sector. It may also be true that the same reasons explain the poor industry response rates to requests for assistance connected to this and other pieces of educational research. It is more likely that sustained increases in student support by industry professionals will be achieved if we reconsider the nature and level of the demands made of them.

Academic perspectives on Foundation degree assessment

The assessment programmes offered by all learning providers surveyed were similar to each other in terms of methods and range of assessment vehicles used. Few institutions had departed from the conventional approaches and those that did used CMC or other on-line approaches to support only a minor part of the assessment. However, the 2004 study indicated a substantial shift in approach with increasingly substantial reliance on the VLE to support summative assessment using interactive multiple choice and short answer question formats. As documented above, academic practitioners' views on employer participation and involvement in assessment were consistently cautious. It was felt by some academics that employers could have a potential role in the assessment of 'generic' skills, which could feed into a professional development module. However it was stressed by these practitioners that reliance on employer testimonials alone would not be sufficient and that performance would need to be further assessed with the help of student analyses, testimonials and commentaries. Some institutions had experience of involving employers in the assessment of the work placement module but none of them attributed weightings of more than 20% to employer feedback. Some respondents shared the view that employers' levels of involvement should be largely confined to 'gentle' monitoring and mentoring. However the 2004 research suggests that perceptions have begun to change significantly with more extensive employer involvement in assessment design and coaching beginning to feature on some programmes.

It was suggested to respondents that students' 'real-life' performance in the work place (e.g. in solving a real life problem relating to operations, human resources or sales) might be linked to assessment in related modules. The earlier research revealed a fairly consistent response to this suggestion was that such an approach would be prone to quality difficulties because of inconsistencies in judgement and variations in the levels of feedback from industry assessors. These considerations, coupled with the time constraints imposed by working patterns and demands in the sector, led to a resounding rejection of this idea by respondents. It was suggested that the only areas where such collaboration might be appropriate was in the area of 'additionality' qualifications such as NVQ Level 3 Hospitality and YMCA trainers' awards. Again the later study and empirical evidence since its completion reflected an attitudinal shift on the education side. This shift possibly related to the QAA's clearly articulated expectation that the Foundation degrees it reviews must demonstrate employer focus and involvement.

Three of the providers surveyed offered 'formative' assessment as part of their programme and in the case of each it was reported that this formative approach had a distinct advantage suited to the needs of the 'new' type of Foundation degree student. Cantwell (2002) asserts that formative assessment should act as a valuable source of feedback to enable students to improve their performance. She draws attention to the QAA code of practice on assessment of students which suggests that institutions should ensure that "appropriate feedback is provided to students on assessed work in a way that promotes learning and facilitates improvement". Price (2003) reminds us that QAA's recommendations can only be effectively followed if assessment strategy is in harmony with other institutional strategies such as human resources and widening participation. The widening participation agenda seeks to engage and develop new types of students including many who have been outside of the education system for a long time. Such students need special support and guidance in areas such as written communication skills and interpretation of assessment criteria. In the earlier stages of their programme it is important that they are not penalised for a lack of knowledge and understanding in the preparation of assessments which more 'conventional' students may regard as routine. Formative assessment provides the opportunity for students to gain confidence and useful feedback before formal summative assessment takes place.

There were some strong views expressed on the benefits and disadvantages of the VLE as a teaching, learning and assessment tool. Many lecturers and course managers asserted that students needed a high level of face-to-face contact during their guided learning hours entitlement. In some areas of the hospitality and leisure sectors students work in small organisations and often in isolation for a large part of the time. It was proposed that such students particularly need the stimulus and group dynamics of face-to-face tuition. Feedback suggested that on-line attendance would be even more problematic than 'conventional' attendance because many students would be prone to give up as soon as they encountered difficulties. One academic observed wryly: "In theory distance learning provision widens participation, in practice it excludes as many students as it includes".

Whilst some providers were sceptical about the potential of VLEs to support students' learning and assessment away from the 'classroom', McGugan (2003) is more optimistic and cites his recent research on the use of asynchronous CMC to improve student support on industrial placements in hospitality. The project was initiated in response to research that shows students are critical of their placement and especially its supervision. Whilst there is a view that non-traditional students' learning styles might better suit more conventional face-to-face tuition, the rationale underpinning this new programme is that it widens participation to participants who are in full-time employment. McGugan (2003) did not propose to use the CMC for communication between employer and student but between student and institution while the student is, in effect, out of reach and potentially isolated from college support. It is arguable therefore that while support offered via a VLE may not or should not replace conventional tutoring, such distance support may be of valuable supplementary benefit.

Higher education programmes offered within further education colleges ('HE in FE') provide empirical evidence that a 'nurturing' model of delivery can empower learners who might otherwise find the more conventional higher education environment intimidating. The further education tradition of offering tuition within smaller groups may support less confident learners. The Foundation degree model does not exclude the delivery of programmes to smaller numbers provided that economies of delivery can be made later. Alternative approaches, such as on-line tuition can enrich students' experience once they have become more familiar with these modes of learning.

Salmon (2002) maintains that it is not the idea of VLEs or CMC that dissuades a student from using either but that it is instead connected to the computer related design concept of 'affordance' ("where the learner can work out what to do next"). She cautions, therefore, that considerable thought be given to the design of the VLE and that the initial design be structured in a coherent and logical manner which considers each stage of the development process through the eyes of the learner. She suggests that organic or haphazard construction of the VLE is a 'recipe for disaster' and conversely emphasises the need for an integrated, learner friendly system.

Computer aided assessment

It has been seen above, that there is a following amongst the academic community who endorse the benefits of learning via a VLE for Foundation degree students. There is also the issue of what type of assessment, if any, should be offered to students within a VLE. Oliver (2000) suggests that typically CAA (Computer Aided Assessment) replaces paper-based examinations. In this instance, the computer displays a number of questions to which the students respond by entering their answers via the keyboard (numerical or textual). The students normally log-on to the system by use of a secure password. The software then stores the student's answers in a secure file format which is then either forwarded to a central database on the departmental server or straight to the involved lecturer. The software should possess the capability to determine the right answers from the student's responses.

Oliver (2000) maintains that the advantages of CAA relate chiefly to factors such as reductions in marking time, improved accuracy of marking, removal of personal bias, the rapid production of statistical information, and provision of immediate, accurate and informative feedback. The disadvantages, however, are well known and relate to issues such as the fact that it is only suitable for questions which require a limited response; it is largely unsuitable, therefore, for subjects such as the Humanities, Business analysis, and Management education; it is difficult to get entirely secure responses; there is a need for a considerable degree of programming expertise and accompanying staff development; and students find prolonged computer work fatiguing. Oliver suggests that CAA should still be adopted but only for those subjects and levels of knowledge assessment to which it is best suited.

General good practice in assessment design and delivery

Whatever particular approach to assessment is taken, it is important to incorporate the general 'wisdom' on good assessment practice presented by such bodies as the QAA and HEFCE. The following checklist summarizes just some of the good practice points relating to assessment design and delivery which are applicable to higher education programmes generally:

- explicit assessment criteria
- consistent application of assessment criteria
- match between assessment and learning outcomes (constructive alignment)
- clearly differentiated grade or mark bandings
- clearly articulated assessment tasks or questions
- consistent oral and written feedback
- prompt turnaround of marked work
- balance and variety of assessment methods .

Brown (2003) asserts that the increased emphasis on student centred learning approaches means that institutions must adapt their assessment strategies accordingly. A student centred assessment programme needs to concentrate on feedback as strongly as on judgement; and assessment must now allow opportunities for reception and remediation within a reasonable timeframe. She also proposes increased use of peer and self-assessment within higher education programmes since these approaches help the student get into the assessment criteria and better understand what they mean.

Student opinions on effective assessment and the appropriateness of a collaborative approach

The primary research into student perceptions of 'effective' assessment focussed on the pilot group of Hospitality Management Foundation degree students at Westminster Kingsway College. Salmon's (2002) criteria for gauging on-line readiness was applied to this group and it was found that all students fell into 'category 2' which meant that students were in need of some preparation and coaching before starting to learn on-line but that all were in possession of basic IT applications skills.

Students were generally very apprehensive about the involvement of their employers in any formalized assessment programme and most voiced their disapproval of this idea in strong terms. Some students commented that they believed that their employers "would not have a clue" how to interpret assessment briefs and would not be interested in learning. All students were, however, open to the idea of encouraging their employers to participate informally in a programme of mentoring and work-based coaching. They were also extremely enthusiastic about the use of CMC within a VLE and the concept of on-line assessment was of interest, although some students expressed concerns about how qualitative assessments such as reports and essays could be marked fairly. The Open University eTMA (Electronic Tutor Marked Assignment) model of feedback was suggested to students as one possible approach to qualitative assessment on-line and students were very positive about the level of feedback and the ability to embed specific tutor comments within the student's assignment .

Staff development

The primary findings from interviews with academic staff corroborate the staff development issues identified in the literature. Most academic staff consulted in institutions offering and/or delivering Foundation degrees expressed concern about the transparency, accessibility and coherence of assessment regulations. Other documentary evidence from assessment briefs collected from various learning providers indicated some discrepancies and inconsistencies in approaches to assessment criteria, grading and assessment decisions. The main concern expressed in relation to staff development amongst course teams was the issue of developing on-line conferencing and assessment skills and the knowledge and skills required to effectively use the VLE. There were specific issues raised regarding the use of assessment software packages and considerable resistance in one learning provider to the introduction of these packages in relation to qualitative assessment.

Conclusions and recommendations

This research study has suggested that the learning and assessment needs of the 'new' Foundation degree student are different in a number of key respects. Many of these differences relate to students' academic background, work commitments and motivation drivers. It is clear that one of the important features that will underpin many courses will be the flexibility of their learning and assessment programmes. Flexibility alone, however, will not guarantee success and there are important quality issues to be considered relating to the development of alternative forms of tutorial support, the creation of appropriate learning materials and the design of assessment systems that drive learning in addition to recognizing achievement. These concluding sections examine the practical implications of meeting the needs of Foundation degree learners and make recommendations to course teams and other practitioners relating to the key themes explored in the study.

Developing an assessment model for hospitality programmes

In general, the findings of this study suggest that assessments should contain formative and summative elements; provide for alternative methods of student-lecturer and student–student interaction; use a variety of delivery vehicles which allow for diverse student entry profiles; and facilitate the involvement of employers as mentors, problem-setters and providers of informal feedback. As well as these general principles of good practice, it has been argued that Foundation degree students have additional needs that require close consideration during the assessment design phase. The additional needs that present significant resourcing challenges include those related to the alleged 'anxious, less bright' characteristics (Smith, 2002) of these 'new' types of student. These challenges are compounded by the fact that students will also have less time available to participate in face-to-face tuition and will be more prone to drop out because of feelings of isolation and anxiety about using other forms of electronic communication.

It is essential, therefore, that communication systems are effective. Regular and timely assessment feedback has been cited by many practitioners and academics as crucial to the progress of less confident students. It has been suggested that 'formative' assessment would be an appropriate vehicle for consolidating learning, offering advice, corrective coaching and encouraging students in a 'non-threatening' way. It is acknowledged that formative assessment may have disadvantages associated with encouraging participation and creating a culture of student dependency. However, such an approach could feature more prominently in the earlier stages of the programme and be incrementally phased out.

Re-iterating the importance of detailed and appropriate assessment feedback, Salmon, (2001) suggests that it is an abandonment of professional responsibility to not give appropriate and timely feedback to students and that where this does not exist course teams need to find ways of creating time for it through 'economies of delivery' (e.g. by using on-line conferencing). Most, if not all, Foundation degree courses will contain an element of face-to-face tuition, although the level of such contact will vary considerably. It is suggested here that course teams capitalize on the initial face-to-face group tutorial contacts to:

- reinforce student confidence
- promote socialization that can be continued on-line
- impart the basic skills of on-line conferencing on an incremental basis
- explain the principles of Foundation degree assessment.

Students who participate in face-to-face tutorials initially are more likely to participate in on-line tutor group activities later in their course; students who do not form the face-to-face tutorial 'bond', however, are significantly more prone to drop out earlier in the programme.

Employer participation in assessment

It has been necessary to revise the hypothesis that a collaborative model of assessment can and should involve hospitality employers in a formal way. In higher education generally, there is a lack of evidence of any initiatives where employers take responsibility for interpreting and applying grading criteria. The primary findings indicated considerable resistance to such 'A' level of collaboration from practitioners in both education and industry sectors. Some institutions report positive but less formalized collaboration on assessment with industry while others cite difficulties with developing mentoring and work-based support for students. It is difficult to envisage the removal of the principal obstacles to employer involvement as they relate to the demanding work endemic within the hospitality sector. It may therefore be useful for providers to consider what nature and level of involvement they can reasonably expect from industry in terms of contribution to the teaching and assessment programme.

The recommendation made here is that providers develop collaborative participation with employers where they can offer tangible rewards to participating companies. These might include the development of work-based live casework where students are actively engaged in analysing problems and devising realistic solutions for employers. Although a seemingly obvious point, providers should consider focusing on cultivating links with organizations that demonstrate willingness to offer their support as opposed to canvassing companies that do not. Dutton et al's (2001) work indicated that a smaller pool of 'co-operative mentor' organizations is preferable to a larger but less supportive bank of employers.

In summary, the findings indicated that the most useful and practicable forms of employer-education collaboration include consultative input on programme design, mentoring support, work placement supervision and the provision of live casework.

Communications systems

It has been argued that supportive, timely and regular communication with students especially during the formative stages of the assessment process is important. Several higher education institutions in the UK - such as the University of Westminster, Queen Margaret University College and Leeds Metropolitan University - are now well advanced in the development of their VLEs. These and other higher education institutions have been successful in encouraging on-line participation to facilitate students' learning and assessment. Salmon's (2002, 2004) work has suggested that the design of the VLE in a coherent and logical manner which focuses on process "through the eyes of the learner" is critical to its success. There is, therefore, a need for institutions to create or acquire an integrated, learner friendly system. It has been seen, however, that there are strongly articulated views (McGugan, 2003, Salmon, 2003) on whether an institution, without the relevant IT technical and curriculum expertise, should attempt to develop its own VLE. It is debatable whether savings generated by internal design and construction would be false economies, particularly if participants fail to use it for the purpose which it was primarily intended for. Salmon (2002) presents a detailed checklist for institutions considering the purchase of a VLE and it is recommended that this and other similar lists be consulted before proceeding further with the development of an on-line learning environment.

In summary the choice of an appropriate VLE to meet the needs of the particular students is paramount. It is therefore recommended that institutions contemplating the design or purchase of a managed VLE should take specialist advice that seeks to incorporate and reconcile the often-conflicting perspectives of pedagogy and technology.

Evaluation of CAA

The existing and potential use of CAA was explored in the research and the findings are presented above. Particular reference was made to Oliver's (2000) work, which explored the benefits and constraints of the range of assessment software packages available. The chief disadvantages cited related to the unsuitability of packages to qualitative assessment in areas such as Humanities and Business education. Oliver maintains that many programmes can usefully assist with formative assessment at more elementary levels (i.e. FE Level 3, HE Level 1) but that it is much more difficult to assess conceptual grasp and application amongst more advanced students. The chief difficulties relate to limitations of potential user response and the inability of programmes to 'read' qualitative responses and make judgements on such submissions.

There is also the issue of conversion of existing assessment formats to those more amenable to CAA such as multiple choice. Such activities are extremely time consuming even for more experienced staff and it is unclear whether such conversions continue to assess learning outcomes as rigorously. Primary research into student preferences in CAA revealed that some students were enthusiastic about the use of CMC and assessment on-line. There were, however, anxieties relating to the fairness and validity of CAA with respect to qualitative work such as reports and essays. The Open University's eTMA model of feedback is one approach to addressing these concerns. The system provides a structured framework within which assignments can be prepared, submitted, collected for marking and returned via a dedicated website to the student. This system does not dispense with the need for a 'marker' or with the need to exercise professional judgement. It does, however, provide the marker with a system where s/he is prompted to provide feedback at regular intervals during the submission. Tracking and record keeping is all handled electronically and there is a minimum need for any of the traditional 'assignment handling' administration.

It is recommended here, therefore, that Foundation degree course teams consider implementing an assessment programme which comprises formative and summative elements. These formative elements could usefully contain forms of 'limited response' on-line assessment. This assessment could be undertaken remotely by students and monitored by the tutor. S/he could then provide advice and corrective guidance to individuals or to the whole tutor group as appropriate. Formative assessment could also extend to qualitative CAA methods so that the student becomes familiar with this form before preparation and submission of summative components. A modified version of the Open University e-TMA system could be used by providers to effectively manage this.

Quality assurance and staff development

A suitable programme of assessment review needs to operate alongside all key stages of the assessment cycle: planning and design, delivery, judgement, feedback and review. Relevant criteria need to be developed which encompass both the existing wisdom on good practice and the specific requirements of assessment. These would include such criteria as effective engagement and motivation of learners via assessment design; vocational relevance; and effective management of the on-line assessment collaboration process. The existing forms of 'assessment review' operated by most institutions could be adapted specifically to reflect the criteria. The key areas of difference from more 'conventional' higher education assessment programmes relate to the monitoring of the tutor's e-moderating skills and on-line assessment. Institutions need, therefore, to adapt their quality systems to take account of this new pedagogical approach. In order for greater transparency, accessibility and coherence of assessment regulations to exist, staff need to have confidence in interpreting the regulations and incorporating them into the design of their assessments. It has been argued that providers should build the necessary time into Foundation degree development sessions on assessment, ideally before programmes commence. A need for development in 'e-moderating' and assessment skills amongst course teams has emerged from the primary research. Effective skills in using the VLE as a teaching and learning environment need to be developed via appropriately qualified facilitators. Salmon (2002) and others have developed models for the development of on-line communication and tutoring skills which rightly emphasize the need for an incremental approach to training both students and academic staff. She also suggests that in order for tutors to become good e-moderators they must first see the VLE as students themselves!

Some reflections on implementing the recommendations

It is easy to recommend good practice but much more difficult to implement it. This final section, therefore, offers some brief personal reflections on the experience of implementing the above research recommendations on a Foundation degree in Hospitality at Westminster Kingsway College. The experience of the programme suggests that there is still considerable resistance from many Foundation degree students to engaging in collaborative activity relating to assessment on-line. This seems to apply to the same extent to peer collaboration, employer-student-collaboration and student lecturer collaboration. The course team has, therefore, been reconsidering how Salmon's (2002) model of on-line socialization can best be applied to the induction stage and the ongoing virtual tutorial support of students. The research suggested that electronic and other forms of distance learning provision may actually decrease participation amongst certain learner groups. Subsequent observation of students has indicated that this phenomenon is by no means exclusive to more mature learners and that young entrants often suffer heightened anxiety relating to VLE use. Therefore in addition to improving the on-line experience, the course team has considered the 'de-webification' of certain subject areas where the previous assumption had been that on-line delivery was appropriate.

A recurrent theme and indicative finding of the study was the benefits of employer involvement in teaching and assessment and the associated challenge of providing tangible motivators to organizations in order to facilitate this. Since the end of the initial study a number of institutions have reported an increased interest and willingness to participate by employers in certain circumstances. Some of the most successful assessment collaborations reported relate to situations where employers have approached educational institutions for advice on specific operational or management issues. In these cases, institutions have designed problem solving casework for students around these and employers and course teams have been collectively involved in the delivery of teaching and coaching sessions and the subsequent judgements for assessment. It has been apparent, from the observations of the course team and others, that the greater the degree of trust between the three stakeholder groups (employers, course team and students) the more fruitful the outcome has been in terms of student achievement and employer satisfaction. Issues such as the sharing of sensitive information and staff satisfaction data need, therefore, to be discussed and agreed at the outset of such collaborative assessment activity. It has also been observed that industry mentorship support is more likely to be offered to students on an individual or group basis if the organization has already been involved with the course in an 'assessment' capacity.

Notes

[1] The QAA identifies, in *its* Foundation degree benchmark statement, that the core features of the qualification should be: employer involvement in course design and delivery; the development of both practical and theoretical skills and the subsequent application of these in the workplace; a 240 credit point course equally distributed at the new higher education Levels 4 & 5; direct articulated progression to final year (honours) undergraduate level if the student desires; flexible provision and delivery modes including on-line learning and work place learning; and delivery partnerships with other educational institutions (QAA, 2004).

[2] This study and the subsequent research project were both made possible by the Higher Education Academy Hospitality, Tourism, Leisure and Sport subject centre via *its* 'Pedagogic Research Fund'. This fund actively supports research into a wide variety of projects relating to curriculum development/implementation, teaching, and learning within the Hospitality, Tourism, Leisure and Sport subject areas.

[3] The formal aims of the research were to: (1) make recommendations for the development of suitable assessment models for the Hospitality Foundation degree building on the existing

principles of vocationally contextualised approaches, (2) propose approaches for the implementation and monitoring of assessment that enrich students' learning which are both academically robust and vocationally relevant, and (3) identify the development and training needs of academic staff and industry participants designing and delivering assessment. This translated into the following objectives: (1) to assess the feasibility, nature and extent of employer involvement in assessment, (2) to develop one possible assessment model for use within Hospitality Foundation degrees, (3) to ascertain the training and development needs of a representative selection of employers, academic staff and students in order to implement such assessment programs, (4) to identify potentially suitable communications interfaces between students, employers and academic staff during the assessment and mentoring process, (5) to assess the role of virtual learning in Foundation degree assessment programmes, *and* (6) to consider the investment in IT systems development that would be necessary to establish such assessment delivery systems.

[4] In addition to the references cited in the text the early literature also includes Rheingold, 1995; Chenault, 1998; Latchem and Lockwood, 1998; Robinson et al., 1998; Cann and Pawley, 1999; Gray and Salmon, 1999; O'Reilly and Morgan,1999; Bakia, 2000; McConnell, 2000; and Preece, 2000. More recently see Been et al, 2001, Churchill et al, 2001, Salmon, 2002, Darby, 2002, Mayes et al, 2002, McGugan, 2003, Seker, 2004, Salmon, 2004, and Parchoma, 2005.

[5] In June 2006, there were considerably more providers offering such programmes: 46 hospitality specific or hospitality related courses are now being offered for the 2006-07 academic year.

[6] This list is based on University of Warwick/HEFCE research presented in the HEFCE Good Practice Series Vol.15: *Supporting higher education in further education colleges.* HEFCE: April 2003.

[7] The Open University's eTMA (electronic Tutor-Marked Assignment) system "allows students to submit written assessments either via the web or by e-mail. Tutors can then access the assignment via the web, mark it online, and submit the marked assignment back. The system records the score and returns the assignment automatically to the student". (Open University, *Glossary of Assessment Terms*,
http://www.open.ac.uk/assessment/pages/glossary-of-assessment-terms.php).

References

Basit, T. (1997) *Research Methods in Education.* Keele Distance Learning Education Publications.

Barnett, B. (1995) 'Developing reflection and expertise: can mentors make a difference?', *Journal of Educational Administration,* v. 33, n.5: pp.45-49.

Bakia, M. (2000) 'Costs of ICT use in higher education: what little we know', *TechKnologia,* v.2, n.1.

Breen, R. et al (2001) 'The role of information and communication technologies in a university learning environment', *Studies in Higher Education,* v.26, n.1.

Burke, R.J. et al (1994) 'Benefits of mentoring in organizations: the mentor's perspective', *Journal of Managerial Psychology,* v.9, n.3.

Brown, G. et al (1997) *Assessing Student Learning in Higher Education.* London: Routledge.

Brown, S. (2003) 'Current trends in assessment in higher education'. Presentation at University of Westminster Teaching and Learning Symposium, 20 May, 2003.

Buswell, J. (2003) 'Constructive alignment in practice'. Presentation at LTSN seminar on assessment, 14 March 2003, Woburn House, London.

Cann, A.J. and Pawley, E.L. (1999) 'Automated online tutorials: new formats for assessment on the WWW', in Brown, S. et al (eds.) *Computer-Assisted Assessment in Higher Education.* London: Kogan Page.

Cantwell, J. (2002)''Formative feedback', *LTSN Link Journal,* Autumn, 2002.

Carruthers, J. (1993) 'The principles and practice of mentoring', in Caldwell, J. and Carter, E. (eds.) *The Return of the Mentor.* London: Falmer Press.

Chenault, B.G. (1998) 'Developing personal and emotional relationships via computer mediated communication', *CMC Magazine,* v. 5, n. 5.

Churchill, E.F., Snowdon, S.N., and Munro, A.J. (2001) *'Collaborative Virtual Environments',* Springer-Verlag, London.

Clutterbruck, D. (1991) *Everyone Needs a Mentor.* London: IPM.

Cotterill, S. (2002) 'Developing and applying assessment criteria in sport: a case study of work-based learning', *LTSN Link Journal,* Issue 5, Autumn, 2002.

Darby, J. (2002) 'Networked learning in higher education: the mule in the barn', in Steeples, C. and Jones, C. (eds.) *Networked learning: perspectives and issues.* Springer-Verlag, London.

DfEE (2000) *Foundation Degrees: a consultation.* Nottingham: DfEE. Available at: http://www.dfes.gov.uk/dfee/heqe/fdcd.htm . Last accessed: 30 June 2006.

DfES (2003) *The Future of Higher Education.* London: DfES.

DfES (2004): *Evaluation of Foundation Degrees: Final Report* DfES/York Consulting Publication date: November 2004.

Dutton, C., Parfitt, G., and Woodward, K., (2001) 'Responding to Dearing through Innovative Learning Strategies: the mentoring of hospitality students by service industry professionals', *Council for Hospitality Management (CHME) Conference Paper, Sheffield 1-2 November 2001.*

Fagenson, E.A. (1989) 'The mentor advantage: perceived career experiences of protégé v. non protégés', *Journal of Organisational Behaviour,* v.10, n.4: 309-320.

Gray, C. and Salmon, G. (1999) 'Academic integrity in electronic universities of the new millennium: a practitioner perspective', *Higher Education in Europe,* v.34, n.2.

Higher Education Council for England (HEFCE, 2003) *Supporting Higher Education in Further Education Colleges: a guide for tutors and lecturers.* Bristol: HEFCE publications.

Jones, P. (2004) 'Finding the hospitality industry? Or finding hospitality schools of thought?' *Journal of Hospitality, Leisure, Sport and Tourism Education,* v.3, n.1, May.

Latchem, C. and Lockwood, F. (eds.) (1998) *Staff Development in Open and Flexible Learning.* Routledge, London

Lockwood, A. (2002) 'Making an exhibition of themselves', *LTSN Link Journal,* Issue 5, Autumn 2002.

Mayes, J., Dineen, F., McKendree, J., and Lee, J. (2002) 'Learning from watching others learn', in Steeples, C. and Jones, C. (eds.) *Networked Learning: perspectives and issues.* Springer-Verlag, London.

McGugan, S. (2001) 'Leadership in a virtual learning environment: assessing the value of computer mediated conferencing', *Council for Hospitality Management Education (CHME) Conference paper.* Sheffield, November 2001.

McConnell, D. (2000) *Implementing Computer Supported Collaborative Learning.* 2nd edition. London: Kogan Page.

McGugan, S. and Pocock, S. (2003) 'On-line support for placement learning: evaluating the potential of a virtual learning environment', Presentation at *Learning and Teaching Support Network (LTSN) Conference,* Sheffield, 11 April 2003.

Moore, S. (2001) *Get Real: work-related teaching and learning.* London: LSDA Publications.

Oliver, A. (2001) 'Computer aided assessment - the pros and cons', Learning and Teaching Development Unit, University of Hertfordshire. Available at http://www.herts.ac.uk/lis/ltdu/learning/caa_procon.htm.

Orpen, C. (1997) 'The effects of formal mentoring on employee work motivation, organizational commitment and job performance', *The Learning Organisation,* v.4, n.2: pp. 53-60.

O'Reilly, M. and Morgan, C. (1999) *Assessing Open and Distance Learners.* London: Kogan Page.

Parchoma, G. (2005) 'Roles and relationships in virtual environments: a model for adult distance educators extrapolated from leadership in experiences in virtual organizations', *International Journal on E-Learning,* v.4, issue 4.

Phillips, M., Lunsford, J., Hawkins, R., and Gilmartin, K. (2000) *Tutoring Online: using CMC to support learning.* Milton Keynes: Open University.

Preece, J. (2000) *Online Communities: supporting sociability and designing usability.* Chichester: John Wiley and Sons.

Price, M. (2003) 'Putting institutional frameworks in place', in *Focus Journal,* June 2003.

QAA (2003) *Report 039: Review of Foundation Degrees.* Gloucester: QAA.

QAA, (2004) *Handbook for the Review of Foundation degrees.* Gloucester: QAA.

QAA (2004)) *Foundation Degree qualification benchmark* Pub. QAA 065 10/2004. Gloucester: QAA.
http://www.qaa.ac.uk/reviews/foundationDegree/benchmark/FDQB.pdf

Rheingold, H. (1995) *The Virtual Community.* London: Minerva.

Rust, C. (2002) 'The impact of assessment on student learning', in *Active Learning in Higher Education.* London: Sage Publications.

Robinson, H., Smith, M., Galpin, F., Birchall, D. and Turner, I. (1998) 'As good as IT gets: have we reached the limits of what technology can do for us?' *Active Learning,* 9, December.

Rogers, J. (2001) *Adults Learning* – 4th edition. Buckingham: Open University Press.

Salmon, G. (2002) *E-tivities: the key to active on-line learning.* London: Kogan Page.

Salmon, G. (2004) *E-moderating.* 2nd edition. Routledge-Falmer.

Seker, J. (2004) *Electronic Resources in the Virtual Learning Environment.* Oxford: Chandos Publishing.

Smith, Brenda, (2002), 'Reviewing assessment to help students learn', *LTSN Link Journal,* Issue 5, Autumn 2002.

Sheehan, C. (2004) 'Hospitality Foundation degrees: aligning delivery models with the widening participation agenda', *Higher Education Academy: Link Journal.* Issue 10, Summer.
http://www.hlst.heacademy.ac.uk/projects/r4_sheehan_summary.pdf

Taylor, S. and Edgar, D. (1996) 'Hospitality research: the emperor's new clothes?', *International Journal of Hospitality Management,* 15, 3: 211-227.

Chapter 6

Foundation Degree and Partnership Approaches to Curriculum Development and Delivery

Mike Doyle
University of Salford

Introduction

The purpose of this chapter is to consider both the tensions and the possibilities of partnership approaches to the development of Foundation degrees. Its focus is a case study of development, and it uses data from a development workshop constructed around the explicit articulation of partner perspectives of priorities for teaching and learning. The premise for this approach is that partnership is conveniently used by policy-makers as the vehicle of delivery, but the processes and tensions in development through partnerships are under-theorised. After contextualizing and describing the case study, this chapter offers an outline of and rationale for the methodology, and then presents and analyses the data. It concludes by offering an analysis framed by Activity Theory (Engestrom, 2001), which sees tensions and conflict in processes of collaboration not as barriers, but as potential catalysts for development.

A case study of development through partnership: a Foundation degree in Community Governance

The partnership consists of a university (specifically a host school for the Foundation degree, Business and Informatics), a servicing School (Environment), the university's education development unit (responsible for widening participation and staff and curriculum development), five of its nine associate colleges, and the local authority employers within which the colleges are located. The university first established links with the colleges in 1993, when it set up its 'Further Education/Higher Education Consortium', a partnership with 35 colleges across the northwest of England, with the purpose of widening access through non-traditional routes into higher education before the HEFCE sponsored widening participation initiatives in 1998. The associate colleges were in effect a distinct group of this Consortium, with which the university had developed stronger and more strategic links.

The university underwent a merger with a local college of technology in 1998. Before this the two institutions had had strong links, with the college being the only associate college of the university at that time. It had adopted the title 'university college' several years prior to merger, and delivered degrees awarded by the university. A bridging unit had been established between the two institutions in 1993 to develop collaborative links with the further education sector through the Consortium. The merger involved the absorption of the college into the new institution, which retained the distinct and strong collegiality of the university. Since the merger the university has been re-organised from eight to four faculties, and 38 departments have been restructured into 15 Schools.

The university is characterised by a highly dispersed 'loosely coupled' (Weick, 1976) managerial framework in keeping with the collegiality characteristic of pre-1992 universities. The Pro-Vice Chancellor (Teaching and Learning), when interviewed, identified the devolution of policy ownership into the newly established faculties and Schools as the biggest challenge to management in such an organisation. Nevertheless the university is proud and respectful of its collegiality, adopting what Trow (1994) classifies as a 'soft managerialism' approach to developments, involving an incremental, devolved approach to change.

The thrust to bid for the Foundation degree prototype came from the educational development unit, which also has responsibility for the university's links with the college sector. It has traditionally initiated, on behalf of the university, new forms of curriculum design and sits at a meso level within the organization between organizational strategy on teaching and learning, and bottom-up delivery within the academic schools. However, as a catalyst for change it is in an unusual position in the university in that it is outside the faculty structure, and therefore has to 'court' the consent of 'host' Schools and their academic communities in engaging in the implementation of initiatives.

In this case the unit, with the Pro-Vice Chancellor, persuaded a School in the Business and Finance faculty to host this development, and used interest from another School, Environment, which deals with employed public sector workers such as housing employees, to service the host School's curriculum. The resulting internal curriculum network has distinct differences, linked largely to professional backgrounds and communities of practice to which the members belonged (Becher and Trowler, 2001; Trowler, 1998).

The colleges are varied in size and identity, but in common is the managerialism based on a dwindling unit of resource. There is one very large mixed-economy college with over 30,000 students, used to delivering higher education courses at all levels, and with franchise relationships with a wide range of universities. There are two urban traditional further education colleges, with a range of levels of teaching from special needs and basic skills to higher level vocational courses. These two are aspirational in terms of their desire to be more 'mixed economy', but geographical limitations of student hinterlands and competition from other colleges means likely expansion will be limited. Nevertheless, the participation in the Foundation degree has marketing advantages for these colleges. The final two colleges are more traditionally sixth form colleges, with an emphasis on 16-19 and 'A' level teaching. One is located in a thriving town between the Merseyside and Manchester conurbations, and the other is in a small town in northeast Lancashire.

Since incorporation in 1993 the colleges have experienced a varying degree of rationalisation of staffing and structures aimed at maximising effectiveness (defined by a range of indicators including cost, performance and retention), and responsiveness to local markets and communities, which have had a marked effect on management style and culture. Staff in the colleges have experienced, to varying degrees, institutional re-organisations, 'downsizing' and redundancy rounds, scathing resource cuts, and requirements to re-apply for posts. Middle managers have throughout been required to take on more responsibility, and the perception of senior managers was that they were responsible for managerial and resource issues focused on 'efficiency' and target-related funding issues, and had little time for curriculum matters.

The employers have had much in common with the college sector, as analysed in Clarke and Newman's (1997) study of public sector management. For example, students in one of the local authorities were all made to re-apply for their posts during the first year of the programme. Such instability created problems not only for the college delivering the programme and the students, but also the commitment from the employer representatives in the development and delivery of the programme. The employers, in keeping with the position outlined by Smith and Betts (2003), demonstrated varying degrees of understanding and commitment to what the whole exercise was about. In only two of the five authorities over the period of the research was there a consistent commitment. Issues such as staff turnover were a major factor in this. Some of the employers, despite consistent overtures, chose to not engage in the process as it developed.

This was not the case in the early stages of collaborating on the bidding process. The employers saw the Foundation degree as serving an important role in professional development for their staff, in response to the government's modernisation agenda. To an extent they responded to the overtures from government and the university, and participated in discussions on the curriculum – to the extent that they insisted on changes to course and module titles (hence a course in Public Administration became Community Governance). However, employer protagonists either moved to other jobs, or became pre-occupied with other issues and therefore became relatively detached.

With the colleges, too, there were difficulties. In one of the sixth form colleges the principal was a key early 'shaper' of the partnership, but on his retirement the new principal saw his strategic focus as being not on higher level courses, but the core 16-19 curriculum. In one of the urban further education colleges the funding model and quality assurance process became an issue. The college was expected to work to university funding and quality assurance systems. For the college this caused operational difficulties, leading to problems between the institutions, particularly for the university, which was responsible for the quality of delivery within the different locations. This reflects the tensions between modes of discursive practices, and in particular between 'management knowledges' and 'professional knowledges', both within and between organisations (Pritchard, 2000: p.29).

Difficulties such as these are inevitable in such a complex partnership development. Sectoral and inter-sectoral partnerships, seen as key units in policy delivery, are expected to and are assumed to be able to operate effectively on a regional basis. Policy-makers and funding bodies, such as HEFCE, make little allowance for local tensions, potential conflict and widening market pressures, in particular between competing further education colleges and employers, in collaborating with a local university. The Foundation degree policy strategy seems essentially based on an approach characterized by instrumental rationality (Sanderson, 1999), premised on an assumption that partnerships between universities, employers and colleges can and will develop and deliver policy.

The literature on collaboration and partnership

The literature on partnership spans four theoretical strands: corporate theory, liberal humanist approaches, complexity theory and critical theory. The positive connotations of 'partnership' are reflected in the largely uncritical, aspirational and even normative nature of much of the literature. This is particularly applicable to corporate theory and liberal humanist approaches. In corporate theory (Thomas, 2002; Huxham, 1993; Pennings, 1981), for example, the rationalist managerialism behind concepts such as 'collaborative advantage' - working together to enhance mutual access to resources and expertise - makes logical sense, but it relies on 'tool-kit' approaches of 'tweaking' inputs to affect outputs, and does not take into account sufficiently issues of power, meaning and interpretation. Liberal humanist approaches (Griffiths, 2000; Clandinin et al, 1993; Somekh, 1994) over-estimate the power of individual autonomy, of agency over structure, and in recognising power differences between partners, are idealistic: it seems sufficient for powerful partners to recognise difference from the outset and make espoused commitments to egalitarian practices.

Where partnership struggles, it is assumed that aims and objectives need further clarification (Milbourne et al, 2003), or more time is needed to build up trust (Trim, 2001), or power differences have not been acknowledged and dealt with from the outset (Griffiths, 2000; Somekh, 1994). The paucity of literature on collaboration and its contextual and development illustrates either consensus on these premises, or that they have not been critically explored. The limited work that has been done (Johnston 1997, Clift et al 2000, Dadds, 1995, James and Worrall, 2000), points to the importance of "acknowledging power differences, status, language, style and purpose, and the building up of strategies to mitigate them" (Griffiths, 2003: pp.102). My contention is that 'partnership' and 'collaboration' are therefore under-theorised, and the literature is to a degree 'captured' by normative and rationalist discourses.

Recently, Warmington et al (2004) have attempted to use theoretical developments in Activity Theory, such as notions of co-configuration and boundary crossing, to frame analyses of inter-professional working in the UK. In doing so they stress 'barriers' identified in more rationalist analyses of partnership (such as Milbourne et al, 2003) should be seen as spaces for dealing with contradictions, conflict and dilemmas, characterized as "double binds" by Engestrom (2001), and therefore as the catalysts for development.

Such an approach has provided the rationale and theoretical framework for the methods used to gather the development data in this paper. The following section briefly summarises this framework, and is essential to an understanding of the methodology.

Analyzing practices of partnership and its development

As partnerships are usually developmental and established for a purpose I have used theories of contextual development of situated practice to frame and analyse my data: in particular Activity Theory (Vygotsky, 1978, Engestrom, 1987, 2001, 2003), and to a lesser extent communities of practice theory (Lave and Wenger, 1991, Lave, 1993 and Wenger, 1998). Both are variants of social practice theory.

Activity theory offers a model, the activity system, (see Figure 1) to frame the design and analyse the development of this partnership. The activity system provides a unit of analysis, and consists of the subjects (the partners) with an object (the broad purpose of the partnership), which is mediated through 'tools' or artefacts (after Vygotsky, 1978). Within the context of this research the subject might be the team or its individual members relating to programme learning outcomes (the object) through the mediating tools of curriculum delivery and assessment, which is subject to rules of quality assurance, and delivered by communities with distinct roles, expertise and functions (such as module leaders, teachers, learning mentors).

It provides a theoretically coherent model for developing practice, incorporating processes of mediation between subjects (partners) and the emerging object, or curriculum, and acknowledges operational contexts, which are rule governed and dependent on divisions of labour. It also provides a conceptual and theoretical basis to analyse 'collaboration' and the emergence of development, or 'expansive' learning. For Blackler (1995), this means that communities may enact new or developing conceptions of their activities, based on challenges rooted in tensions.

Engestrom (2001) also incorporates collaborating activity systems, or partnerships, and further develops the concept of expansive learning, which he (op.cit, 138) equates to Bateson's (1972) 'Learning III': "where a person or group begins to radically question the sense and meaning of the context and to construct a wider alternative context". It provides in this research context a means of conceptualising transition and development within the, at times, contested practices of the collaborators. Questioning of consensus, consciousness of contradiction and its articulation within the activity system, or partnership, form the basis of development and, more significantly, transformation. Such tensions in partnership are conventionally described as barriers. The theoretical issue for development through partnership then becomes one of crossing or dealing with boundaries in complex interacting partner relationships.

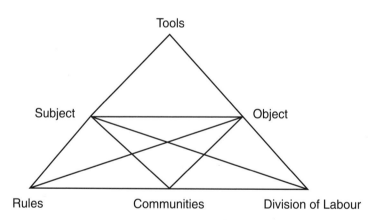

Figure 1: The activity system (after Engestrom, 1987)

The sequence for expansive learning through collaborative boundary crossing is that contradictions within the partnership provide the dynamic for the questioning, remodelling and evaluation of practices (Engestrom, 1999), and this process may result in expansive learning for partners – knowing is constituted through collective, emerging practice. Engestrom refers to the process of expansive learning through working professional groups as 'radical exploration':

> "... radical exploration is learning that is not yet there. It is creation of new knowledge and new practices for a newly emerging activity, that is, learning embedded in and constitutive of the qualitative transformation of the entire activity system". (Engestrom, 2004: p.4)

Method of data collection

Data for this research has been collected through a combination of interviews with partners from the three constituencies, interspersed with developmental workshops, or as Engestrom et al (1995) call them: 'boundary crossing laboratories'. These were based on the interventionist concept of Development Work Methodology, or DWM (Engestrom, et al 1995), a method particularly suited to insider-research, and the research of emerging processes. Traditional research methods involve the researcher observing the subjects of the research at a distance. Development Work Methodology, in contrast, involves interventions by the researcher, usually in the form of providing spaces or fora for the research subjects to engage in dialogue linked to the development of a shared interest, such as a project. The sequence is illustrated in Figure 2. Data was also available from participant observation in other formal and informal team meetings, such as steering group meetings and boards of examiners.

Individual interviews were held at the end of semester one for intake one. Amongst the data gathered were two issues – individual perspectives on priority learning goals for the programme, and having experienced the first semester, changes required for the next intake of students to enhance delivery of those learning goals. This data from the interviews, made anonymous, was used as a stimulus at the start of the first developmental workshop. For the purposes of this chapter I summarise the outcomes of the initial development workshop to provide the context for the data analysis of the second workshop a year later. The starting point for the second workshop was a review of the outcomes agreed a year earlier.

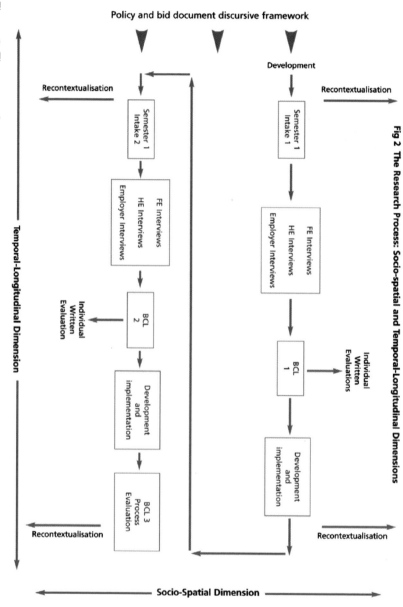

Figure 2: The research process

Example of data and analysis

Summary of first development workshop

The first workshop was structured broadly around Engestrom's (1999) expansive learning cycle phases of questioning, analysing and modelling. I called these 'what' issues (those raised in the interviews), 'why' issues (discussion between the partners on the 'what' issues), and moved from these to thinking about 'how' issues for the second intake of students (Engestrom's process of 'modelling'). Subsequent phases of the cycle are examining the model, implementing it, consolidating and evaluating. The process of evaluation is also one of questioning – hence the notion of expansive 'cycle'.

In my initial data analysis each of these three segments broke down into distinct episodes: under 'what' issues, discussion ranged from the intended work-based nature of the learning to a tendency towards 'academic drift', to the problems deliverers of the curriculum in the colleges were facing operating within university practices and quality systems in different institutional settings.

Discussion within the 'why' episodes was more open and in the second of these, on assessment, college staff and the employer representative challenged modular practices and initiated processes of modelling rooted in their own situated practices, involving propositions to integrate assessment across modules. There were a number of attempts by college tutors to 'stabilize' debate (Engestrom, 2004 p.139) and anchor propositions in order to 'normalize' practice at this stage and move forward, but these did not involve attempts at boundary crossing – rather they represented assertions of challenge to dominant university practices. The notion of boundary crossing is interesting in partnership formation and development.

Its roots are in Engestrom, Engestrom and Karkkainen's (1995) recognition of emerging multi-professional working practices, a 'new work paradigm', when they developed the notion of a horizontal sharing of expertise and understanding ('collective concept formation', op.cit: 329) across activity systems. 'Polycontextuality', as they refer to it, recognised that:

> "... experts operate in and move between multiple parallel activity contexts...(which) demand and afford different, complementary, but also conflicting cognitive tools, rules and patterns of social interaction...Experts face the challenge of negotiating and combining ingredients from different contexts to achieve hybrid solutions". (op.cit: p.319)

The issue then became one of crossing boundaries in complex interacting activity systems to achieve such hybrid solutions. Engestrom (2004) claims that in developing practices between activity systems, expansive learning should be reformulated as 'boundary crossing actions'.

The 'how' phase of modelling, discussing options for moving things forward for the next student intake, was characterized by boundary tensions rooted in a range of issues. These can be summarized as contested priorities: for the higher education staff it was consistency, timing and quality of delivery, and knowledge transfer to deadlines circumscribed within modular 'containers'. For the further education tutors it was diagnosing learner starting points, knowledge construction and skills development as the pedagogical priority, with whole programme, rather than modular perspectives. For the employers, priorities were corporate human resource targets. Boundaries were exposed in the workshop, if not crossed, but compromises were reached on four issues for the second intake: thematic approaches to assessment within semesters with skills embedding; cross-modular themes that make sense to the students; personal development planning to be introduced from induction; and university module leaders to be responsible for staff development for module teams across the colleges.

To an extent there were attempts throughout the workshop to stabilise the debate and reach consensus on meanings and proposed practices. The programme leader recognised the rationale for linking assessment between modules within semesters, and if possible across semesters. However, in doing so this posed no threat to the autonomy of the modular structure and the module leaders. Was the experience expansive for the partnership? This was unlikely at this stage in the development process. Nevertheless, the distributed nature of knowledge and expertise did have an impact in that assessment patterns were changed for the second cohort of students, and higher education staff were to a degree responsive to the problems of curriculum delivery articulated by those with its responsibility.

Analysis of the second development workshop

The collaborative practice, a further year on, was still characterised by hierarchies in terms of roles, and culture clashes of further education college teachers used to operating within clearly managed practices having to relate to relatively autonomous module leaders at the university. However, there was a greater self-confidence and recognition by the college teachers of their identity and expertise, with the kind of students on this Foundation degree – employed, part-time adult-returnees. A key issue throughout had been the higher education tutors' emphasis on knowledge transfer, particularly the volume, and the practicalities, for the 'teacher-labourers' in the colleges, of meeting the needs of learner diversity in three hours per week (this metaphor came from the interview data with the college tutors, and reflects perceptions of their positioning by others within the partnership – particularly university staff and the programme leader). Engestrom (2001) refers to such contradiction and tension as the double bind that provides the catalyst for change. Different perspectives and priorities for the four identified targets were clear, and rooted in divisions of expertise and professional interest. For example, while there had been developments in cross-modular themes and assessment, little development had taken place in personal development planning, and the colleges had either developed their own systems, or had adapted existing college practices. Different perspectives and motivation by the subjects (partners) in conceptualising the object (for example, further education priorities of learner development in contrast with the higher education priority of covering the material) provide a clear boundary that either has to be crossed, or at least accommodated.

This double bind appeared very early in the second development workshop. The contradiction, interestingly, was championed by the clear opinion leader for the college lecturers. She (I will call her Susan) was experienced in delivering higher level work in a mixed economy college, and throughout the exchanges in the workshop, particularly in the questioning phase, her leadership of her other college partners at the boundaries being confronted was recognised and supported by them. The division of labour between writing and delivering modules was raised by Susan:

> *Try teaching what you are writing and then work out how you need to change it … it's handed down , and unless you actually go in and try to teach it to the type of students that are coming into the college three hours a week …try to deliver this module to them yourself.*

When the Programme Leader (PL) responds with a question about how the problem might be resolved, Susan, with the enthusiastic support of one of the employers, responds by inviting him into her college to teach the module. The PL recognises the value of this but raises the 'practicalities' of resources, time and other constraints. While acknowledging these, a university tutor from a servicing School, Jean, acknowledges to Susan that she is right. Another of the further education tutors, Ruth, then validates Susan's assertions:

> *The module leaders' expectations are unrealistic. They are not aware of the problems that you are facing with that particular type of learner.*

Susan develops this theme by demonstrating how she adapts the material, adds to it and prioritises it in the learners' interests:

> *… adapting what you have been given…to suit the students. You supplement it in ways the students can understand".*

Such assertion of professional priorities, expertise and practice encourages Ruth to share:

> *I might go in one week and decide that I will completely change the next sessions because I have noticed they have missed something.*

The dialogue represents an emerging positioning of the college voice in this context. The other three college tutors lend their support through reinforcing verbal comment and non-verbal signals, supporting the data picked up in the individual interviews prior to the workshop.

This culminates in Susan's categorical assertion:

> *You have to go where they want to take you, because it's important to them...you might start off with something that dominates the whole of the class because they want to talk about it, they want to relate it back to their experience...you have to go with that...that's given them something to bring back to the next session: it's about flexibility, but that isn't implied within the modules.*

This episode of questioning represents a tension rooted in epistemologies and pedagogies, and is the result of conflict within the activity system culminating in this double bind. In Engestrom's terms this is a potential turning point where something has to give for development, or expansive learning to take place. The PL's response effectively opens the way to the phase of analysis and modelling, in the expansive cycle, in moving the development forward:

> *In listening to that I am thinking increasingly that the sessions at the colleges shouldn't be so rigid.*

Susan's response is a plea for reciprocity and a recognition of expertise:

> *You have to have a structure... I think at the local level we have to take that on-board...where at the chalk face we are delivering it, we are getting to know what works and what doesn't. If we feed that back (to the module leaders) they need to take that on-board, and not say 'no you can't'...not that they have.*

The phase of modelling in this case represents a process of accommodation around contested discursive practices. The critical issues for the university staff reflect epistemological and pedagogical issues of knowledge transfer, quality (Jean refers to 'ironing out variation'), and assessment practices within modular structures. Recognition of the constraints in the colleges results in a proposal by the PL, supported by Jean, for more of the delivery to be done at the university sessions (all Foundation degree students at the colleges attend the university for two days each semester).

The dialogue in this phase reflects positions characteristic of individual practices. For the PL this means:

> *I would need a full day and an evening to deliver significant parts of Asset Building.*

Jean's response is:

> *We'll have to be flexible for different modules – you couldn't talk at someone for three hours.*

The needs of the learner are a priority for Susan. She stresses that in induction links between assessment and themes in the first semester should be clarified for the students – 'you know, lay it down for them'. At this Jean expresses surprise, thinking they had been made clear following the actions agreed at the first development workshop. This illustrates the distributed nature of knowledge in collective developmental practices, and the significance of learning as a social process (Lave, 1993).

The process of accommodating perspectives and priorities through modelling leads gradually to attempts to stabilize the debate and agree to normalize the practice of more delivery at the university. This meets university priorities, and is wrapped by Jean in a way that accommodates the college tutors' priority of supporting the learner:

> *I mean it must be difficult for them (further education tutors) to have that concrete information in their handbooks and not really have the forum to deliver it in. I don't know how you get round that.*

The PL agrees, commenting that an hour and a half per week for each module is inadequate. Susan responds by explaining that in some sessions 'we started doubling up as it was the only way you could continue it through'.

This jockeying for consensus results in a critical moment in the dialogue at the boundary:

> Jean: *So that would work from your point of view – to have more formal delivery at the university?*

> Susan: *I think when they come into the university and you do keynote lectures to them, I think that would be useful.*

Susan's position as opinion leader is endorsed by Ruth:

> *I think that as a lecturer that gives you a point to aim at.*

However, Susan does express reservations that it 'would not sort everything', particularly across the other colleges, where she says 'I don't know whether they are all doing something different'. Whether this is consensus or reluctant acquiescence is uncertain at this stage.

The division of labour (and status and power) was clear throughout the whole process of development researched, and the frustration expressed by the colleges and to a lesser degree the employer reflected the dominant discourses to which they were required to adapt. Their frustration is reminiscent of Wenger's assertion of the need for negotiability of meaning in such collaborative activity:

> "When in a community of practice the distinction between production and adoption of meaning reflects enduring patterns of engagement among members – that is, when some always produce and some always adopt – the local economy of meaning yields very uneven ownership of meaning. This situation, when it persists, results in a mutually reinforcing condition of both marginality and inability to learn."
> (Wenger, 1998: p.203).

Wenger is essentially arguing for recognition of expertise within the division of labour in the partnership, of give and take. For the college staff to operate within prevailing university practices and rules with no opportunity to impact on them is counter-productive, and will stifle development. Positions adopted through the development workshops do indicate gradual transition resulting from the bottom up, with the colleges' more constructivist, learner centred pedagogic approach resulting in effective challenges to the more traditional university approaches of knowledge transfer. However, this occurred over a full two-year period, indicating that time and the formation of relationships are important factors in advancing change. It would appear to represent 'hybridity' and boundary crossing as a gradual process of mutual learning and accommodation, one of movement and transformation, understanding and even experiencing others' worlds.

The notion of the activity system (Figure 1) in this case needs to accommodate diversity of subject (partner) perspective and motive in framing the object. The outcomes of development workshop two represent an accommodation of motives around conceptualizations of the object (learner development needs in contrast to covering the material). Compatibility was critical in this case, ensuring development in ways that satisfied the different partners. For the college partners, this means that their priorities of skills diagnosis, personal development planning, and knowledge construction on a whole programme basis match the expertise they bring and roles they expect to fulfil within the partnership. For the university tutors, priorities of knowledge transfer, assessment, quality and consistency were also accommodated.

This analysis is in keeping with the views of Nardi (2005) and Kaptelinin (2005). Nardi demonstrates how even in a single company, an object of activity was shared between members of a research department, but that this was in tension with the company management's priorities. However, both were able to work to the same ends through distinct but compatible motives.

Tensions, difficulties and barriers associated with partnership working, particularly in the rationalist and liberal humanist literatures, are constructed as issues to be resolved through effective planning or goodwill. These conditions of interagency working are usually the norm, and while planning and relationship building is important, the constructive and developmental nature of process, and movement through dealing with contradictions and tension, are critical to progress. The initial questioning in Engestrom's cycle, and the creation of time and space for it to happen, provides the dynamic for development, change and boundary crossing.

The evidence from this experience is that boundaries were accommodated. Within the activity system, this experience demonstrates that the object of the collaboration is multi-faceted, and for it to act as a system, the positions and perspectives of the subjects on the object have to be accommodated throughout the expansive phases of development. Hence contested priorities and conceptualizations of learning, issues of skills or content, modes of delivery, didactic transfer or knowledge construction through personal development planning, modes of assessment, modules or whole programme approaches are sites where collaborators have to address incompatibilities for progress to occur.

Such development requires positions and perspectives to be articulated and listened to. The issue of power and opportunities to contest hegemonies within this process is critical to progress.

Lessons for partnerships?

Making partnerships more effective needs the articulation of interest, difference, perspective and interpretation explicitly from the outset. This needs to initiate a process of reflexivity that requires partners within the activity, regardless of status, to articulate their object, or purpose, which may vary between partners. This needs to be recognised and appropriate priorities, compatibilities and compromises negotiated from the beginning, and subsequently throughout the process. The notion of 'collaborative advantage' should be contextualised in determining the realisation of interpretation of goals for partners, and the potential of the process for (distributed) knowledge construction through practice needs to be monitored reflexively.

As the earlier quote from Wenger observes, negotiability is critical in having a stake in the enterprise. Rationalist goals for partnerships need to be adaptable to accommodate perspective and the more broadly situated development process. This requires recognition that such goals may change, or need to be adapted when contextualised. It is the development process that is critical in constituting the identity and realisation of such emergent goals, and provision needs to be made for reflexivity and ownership within the process. Tensions, difference and contested ground should not be conceptualized as barriers to development. Rather, space and time need to be built into developmental processes to enable such double binds to act as catalysts for the realization of expansive potential.

References

Bateson, G. (1972) *Steps to an Ecology of Mind.* New York: Ballantine Books.

Blackler, F. (1995) 'Knowledge, knowledge work, and organization: an overview and interpretation', *Organization Studies* 6: 1021-46

Becher, T., and Trowler, P. (2001) *Academic Tribes and Territories: intellectual enquiry and the cultures of disciplines.* Buckingham: SRHE/OUP.

Clandinin, D. J., Davies, A., Hogan, P. and Kennard, A. (eds.) (1993) *Learning to Teach, Teaching to Learn. Stories of collaboration in teacher education.* New York and London: Teachers College Press.

Clarke, J. and Newman, J. (1997) *The Managerial State.* London: Sage

Clift, R., Allard, J., Quinlan, J. and Chubbock, S. (2000) 'Partnerships are mortal: debunking the myth of partnership as the answer for improving education'. In M. Griffiths and G. Impey (eds.) *Working Partnerships: better research and learning.* Nottingham: Nottingham Trent University.

Dadds, M. (1995) *Passionate Enquiry and School Development: a story about teacher action research.* London: Falmer.

Engestrom, Y. (2004) 'New forms of expansive learning at work: the landscape of co-configuration'. Paper presented to the LSE Department of Information Systems *ICTs in the contemporary world: work management and culture* seminar. 22 January 2004.

Engestrom, Y. (2003) 'The horizontal dimension of expansive learning: weaving a texture of cognitive trails in the terrain of health care in Helsinki'. In F. Achtenhagen and E.G. John (eds.) *Milestones of Vocational and Occupational Education and Training. Volume 1: The teaching-learning perspective.* Bielefeld: Bertelsmann.

Engestrom, Y.E. (2001) 'Expansive learning at work: toward an activity theoretical reconceptualisation', *Journal of Education and Work,* 14, 1: 133-155.

Engestrom, Y. (1999) 'Innovative learning in work teams: analyzing cycles of knowledge creation in practice'. In Y. Engestrom, R. Miettinen and R-L. Punamaki *Perspectives on Activity Theory.* Cambridge: CUP.

Engestrom, Y.E., Engestrom, R., and Karkkainen, M. (1995) 'Polycontextuality and boundary crossing in expert cognition: learning and problem solving in complex work activities', *Learning and Instruction,* v.5: pp 319-336.

Engestrom, Y. (1987) *Learning by Expanding: an activity-theoretical approach to developmental research.* Helsinki: Orienta-Konsultit.

Griffiths, M. (2003) *Action for Social Justice in Education.* Maidenhead: OUP.

Griffiths, M. (2000) 'Collaboration and partnership in question: knowledge, politics and practice'. *Journal of Education Policy,* 15, 4: 383-395

Huxham, C (1993) 'Collaborative capability: an intra-organisational perspective on competitive advantage', *Public Money and Management,* July-September, pp. 21-28.

Kaptelinin, V. (2005) 'The object of activity: making sense of the sense-maker', *Mind, Culture and Activity,* v.12, n.1: 4-18.

James, M. and Worrall, N. (2000) 'Building a reflective community: development through collaboration between a higher education institution and one school over 10 years', *Educational Action Research,* v.8, n.1: 93 -114.

Johnston, M. (ed.) (1997) *Contradictions in Collaboration: new thinking on school/university partnerships.* New York: Teachers College Press.

Lave, J. (1993) 'The practice of learning'. In S. Chaiklin and J. Lave (eds.) *Understanding Practice: perspectives on activity and context.* Cambridge: CUP.

Lave, J., and Wenger, E. (1991) *Situated Learning: legitimate peripheral participation.* Cambridge: CUP.

Milbourne, L., Macrae, S. and Maguire, M. (2003) 'Collaborative solutions or new policy problems: exploring multi-agency partnerships in education and health work', *Journal of Education Policy,* v.18, n.1: 19-35.

Nardi, B. (2005) 'Objects of desire: power and passion in collaborative activity', *Mind,Culture and Activity,* v.12, n.1: 37-51.

Pennings, J. M. (1981) 'Strategically interdependent organisations'. In Nystrom, P.C. and Starbuck,W. H. (eds), *Handbook of Organisational Design.* Oxford: Oxford University Press.

Pritchard, C. (2000) *Making Managers in Universities and Colleges.* Buckingham: SRHE/OUP.

Sanderson, I. (1999) 'Participation and democratic renewal: from 'instrumental' to 'communicative rationality' ?', *Policy and Politics,* v. 27, n.3: 325-341.

Smith, R. and Betts, M. (2003) 'Partnerships and the consortia approach to United Kingdom Foundation degrees: a case study of benefits and pitfalls', *Journal of Vocational Education and Training,* v.55, n.2: 223-240.

Somekh, B. (1994) 'Inhabiting each other's castles: towards knowledge and mutual growth through collaboration', *Educational Action Research,* v.2, n.3: 357-381.

Trim, P.R.J. (2001) 'An analysis of a partnership arrangement between an Institute of Further Education and an Institute of Higher Education', *Journal of Further and Higher Education,* v.25, n.1: 107-116.

Thomas, E. (2002) 'Collaboration within and between HEIs in England: a review of policy and practice'. In E. Thomas, M. Cooper and J. Quinn (eds.) *Collaboration to Widen Participation in Higher Education.* Stoke-on- Trent: Trentham Books.

Trow, M (1994) 'Managerialism and the academic profession: the case of England'. *Higher Education Policy,* v. 7, n. 2: 11-18.

Trowler, P. (1998) *Academics Responding to Change: new higher education frameworks and academic cultures.* Buckingham: SRHE/OUP.

Vygotsky, L. S. (1978) *Mind in Society: the development of higher psychological processes.* Cambridge, MA: MIT Press.

Warmington, P., Daniels, H., Edwards, A., Brown, S., Leadbetter, J., Martin, D., and Middleton, D. (2004) *Interagency Collaboration: a review of the literature.* ESRC: TLRP III. Accessed 20 March 2005.

Wenger, E. (1998) *Communities of Practice: learning, meaning and identity.* Cambridge: CUP.

Weick, K.E. (1976) 'Educational organizations as loosely coupled systems', *Administrative Science Quarterly,* v.21, n.1: 1-19.

Chapter 7

Work-based Learning and Foundation Degrees

EXPLORING ASSESSMENT AS AN ACTIVE PROCESS OF STUDENT CHOICE AND ENGAGEMENT

Laurence Solkin
City University

Introduction

This chapter explores the influence of assessment at work on learning within the context of a Foundation degree. Starting with the idea that the curriculum is driven by the assessment process, and taking inspiration from David Boud's proposition that "work is the curriculum" (Boud 1998), it seeks to explore firstly, how the curriculum can be inferred from the assessment process and, more broadly, how learning is influenced by work place assessment. Assessment is significant in two senses: firstly, as a means of demonstrating success and, secondly, as an indicator or reflection of the curriculum itself, i.e. what is actually being learned at work. To this extent the assessment of work-based learning should reflect the curriculum of work and also validate individual learning. If we accept Challis's point that employers "have first-hand knowledge about what makes for good performance amongst their employees" (Challis, 2005: p. 10) the key questions for educational providers become 'what do current workplace assessment processes tell us about what employers want?' and 'how is this perceived (or experienced) by learners themselves?' The incorporation of learning at, or derived from, work is a key component of Foundation degrees:

> "Work-based learning programmes have... been developed from school to postgraduate and continuing professional development levels in response to government initiatives on vocational education and social inclusion. Foundation degrees epitomise this tendency as a form of higher education provision which is vocationally focused but which integrates work-based and higher level academic learning. Work-based learning is, therefore, one of the core characteristics of Foundation degrees as defined by QAA in its Foundation degree benchmark statement." (*fdf In Brief: Work Based Learning:* p.1)

If Foundation degrees are seen to "fit perfectly into the world of work" (ibid) then this fit should be reflected within the assessment process at work.

Work-based learning has focused on introducing work into academia and creating programmes, with employers, which both recognise and utilise the work environment as part of the learning process. In seeking to do so some writers have tended to regard learning in the work environment as a 'given' – part of "a naturally-occurring curriculum of experience" (Moore 2004). This may well be true but only at what Beaney describes as "the trivial level where some form of learning is derived from almost any form of experience" (Beaney, 2004: p. 8). More critical approaches to work-based learning have tended to question the naturalness of the learning process and in doing so explore how academic learning and work practices can both reinforce and compete with each other.

Work-based learning is often discussed in relation to the concept of a 'community of practice' (Lave and Wenger, 1991) which is constructed through the activities and practices which participants engage in on a regular basis. Novice learners start out on the margins of such communities but as their participation in the community, and consequently their knowledge, grows they locate themselves more centrally within it. Fuller and Unwin (2003) describe this as "a clearly defined and bounded linear journey in which old timers train and mould their successors, thus ensuring the continual reproduction of an organisation or community of practice". Although the idea of a community is not central to this study, their research sheds some light on the nature of the community and the journeys made within it. For Hennessy and Sawchuck (2003) the opportunity to learn is governed by the status of the worker and is directly linked to their social status. As such, it is affected by the specific characteristics of the individual learner including class, gender, ethnicity and age. Huzzard (2004) adds to this the specific position of the learner within the work place as a community of power distinguishing between 'sensemaking', as a process of creating personal mental representations, and 'sensegiving', in which the dominant group provides meaning for those who are subordinate. The status of learners within the process of work-based assessment is therefore also significant. For Billet (2004) social structure provides only part of the answer as engagement at work is also a function of individual agency and intentionality and "individuals sometimes elect to dis-identify with social practices in which they engage" (Billet, 2004: p.320). Such a process of engagement and disengagement could be used to explain how learners present or locate themselves within the assessment process.

The relationship between the assessment of work performance and learning is also problematic. Fuller and Unwin's (2003: p.41) consideration of engineering apprenticeships illustrates some of the constraints and tensions within the apprenticeship process. Whilst arguing that the apprenticeship system "has always been concerned with personal (long-term) as well as job specific (short-term) development" (ibid p.42), they go on to note that the production imperative means that if "the smooth execution of production requires an apprentice to spend all his (sic) time operating and, therefore becomes an expert in running one or two machines, then this is what happens" (ibid, p.44). By extension, therefore, the appropriate measure of competence in this context would be derived from the ability to operate two machines rather than a broader definition of the role of the accomplished expert. This notion of partial or 'expedient competence' is embedded in the requirements of work, i.e. competence is defined by, and subsequently defines, the performance domain. In this sense performance-based systems at work could be seen to restrict learning by privileging the tactical at the expense of the strategic and the immediate at the expense of the long term.

Assessment

As educators we are familiar with an emphasis on the assessment process as part of learning design. The significance of assessment within higher education has been highlighted by many authors (Elton and Laurillard, 1979; Crooks, 1988; Shepard, 2000). Ramsden, for example, argues that "from our students' point of view, assessment always defines the actual curriculum" (2003: p.187) - which suggests that the assessment process can be used to drive the curriculum. This is echoed by Biggs (2003) who reminds us that: "To the teacher, assessment is at the end of the teaching-learning sequence of events, but to the student it is at the beginning" (2003: p.141). According to one set of researchers: "students often work 'backwards' through the curriculum, focusing first and foremost on how they will be assessed and what they will be required to demonstrate they have learned" (CSHE, 2006). To many practitioners assessment is the cornerstone on which the edifice of higher education rests as "assessment is the most powerful lever teachers have to influence the way in which students respond to courses and behave as learners" (Gibbs, 1999: p.41).

Assessment at work can be seen as having growing significance for performance but less obvious links to learning. Formal assessment is normally associated with the process of performance management and typically includes some form of appraisal. Fletcher and Williams (1992) argued that the appraisal system was a product of the "social, political and psychological beliefs of its time" (1992: p.13) - to which one might add the influence of specific organisational context. Historically, the literature on appraisal has been characterised by dilemmas between development and reward, between the involvement of managers and the reliability of managerial judgement, and between local autonomy and organisational control (Hall et al, 2004). More recently, however, the dominance of the performance management paradigm within human resources practice (Hendry et al, 2000) has focused attention at the organisational level with an attempt to translate organisational targets and values into individual systems. As Simmons points out "contemporary performance management systems and prescriptive literature in performance management emphasise the control aspect of appraisal by specifying and measuring the individual's contribution to the organisation as a whole" (2002: p.88). Despite this the views of those who are appraised suggest that issues around consistency and favouritism (Armstrong and Baron, 1998) remain, as well as problems over translating complex organisational strategy into individual targets or goals (Hendry et al, 2000). If we, as educational providers, are to understand what employers want we must be able to interpret these systems (including the dilemmas which they reflect) and analyse their role within the learning process.

The research process

The research is both purposeful and opportunistic. Purposeful in the sense that it is directly linked to the process of course evaluation and opportunistic in that it is situated within an ongoing process of teaching and learning. The research methodology can be described as mixed in that it seeks to combine two different methodological positions or discourses – regulatory positivism (in the form of a questionnaire) with a more discursive or interpretive approach (using focus groups and students' own reflective assignments). The questionnaire aimed to identify what aspects of performance were being assessed at work, whilst the focus groups explored how the assessment process operated or was managed and what part was played by the learners themselves. The data is derived from over 12 full-time and part-time Foundation degree students undertaking a course in public service management. The sample is convenient, being composed of students on a specific Foundation degree at a given institution.

Results

Questionnaire data was used to explore the fit between academic and work place assessment and in particular the extent to which different domains were assessed within different systems. The most obvious lack of fit related to the perception of theory and knowledge within the work place. The academic assessment system privileges knowledge generally and theory in particular to an extent that was not replicated at work. Although 'knowledge' was seen by learners as part of the perceived assessment process at work, the type of knowledge related to an understanding of other, similar organisations and in particular the experience of other organisations' activities such as managing change. Learners received recognition not from theory but through their knowledge of other organisations' practice. This preference for practical or case-based knowledge could be expressed explicitly but more often was seen as part of a culture which perceives theory as abstract or irrelevant to day to day management practice. Pragmatic knowledge was seen as more available and useful to practising managers and therefore preferred by work-based assessment systems.

The area of diversity and diversity management also provided some interesting comparisons. Whilst diversity was seen as a key element in the academic assessment process, this was less true of work-based systems. Although the public services are strongly committed to diversity management at a policy level, it does not seem that this area is currently included within the assessment of managers. Diversity was seen as of little significance to the assessment of management performance and learners commented that this aspect of organisational policy or values was rarely assessed. Some students were deeply critical of their own organisations' commitment in this area and pointed to the contradictions between having a strong policy statement but relatively little interest in managers and their practice.

The lack of consistency between, and sometimes within, organisations was also noted with some cultures operating within strict definitions of performance and others employing a broader but more implicit set of criteria. This variability was most noticeable in discussion around the focus of the appraisal in relation to some organisations having a closely defined approach and others employing a more developmental one. One participant described the entire process within her organisation as 'completely haphazard', with different processes and criteria in operation at the same time without any real sense of direction or coherence. The variability of assessment content between employers within a single sector was considerable.

Comparing the area of 'learning' also produced some interesting results in terms of managing one's own learning. Despite several positive comments regarding supportive learning cultures, this area was seen as of low significance within the context of work place assessment. Again there was a mismatch between the explicit commitments made by public sector organisations to self development and their operation within the assessment system. Where self development was seen as a significant factor this often was accompanied by a change in the assessment process with greater reliance on the employee planning their own learning and claiming achievements rather than being a passive recipient of an assessment. In some cases, however, the assessment of the learning domain was completely absent, suggesting a narrow focus on specific performance.

Work-based assessment also seemed to be less significant in terms of assessing group processes and group dynamics, although this was balanced, in some cases, by a more specific focus on leadership behaviours and the social role of the leader. At first sight, this may seem contradictory, in as much as becoming skilled in managing group processes is seen as common to group membership as well as group leadership. On the other hand, it may suggest that staff were not being assessed in relation to their participation within groups unless they were the designated leader of the group. Work-based assessment valued practical problem solving in contrast to a deeper understanding of the social or political context. Criteria related to practical problem solving at a tactical level tended to be more significant at work than an understanding of public service management in general. Responses in this area may well reflect the work status of the respondent rather than a universal approach to managing within the public sector, i.e. that a more strategic approach is expected of a more senior manager. Taken together these two aspects of work place assessment suggest that status is a significant factor in how learners are assessed at work. Whilst not conclusive, the overall data also suggests the dominance of specific performance and a preference for short-term immediate results.

In exploring the process of work place assessment, the research revealed the operation of two parallel and interlinked approaches: a formal system focused around a regular appraisal cycle and an informal system operating on a day to day level. For the most part the formal process of assessment at work consisted of target setting and annual appraisal. Target setting was seen as part of a hierarchical process with service delivery targets being translated into group and personal objectives. Although it was possible to translate some service targets into specific performance measures it is difficult to map these onto managerial roles or activities. At best these targets provided a broad context within which individual performance would be assessed rather than specific measures or criteria. By contrast the process of appraisal was much more personalised. The periodic review of performance focused on the individual and although service targets were used to derive annual objectives space was also provided to include personal objectives in the form of learning or development needs.

In addition to the formal system, learners also identified a range of informal processes which informed day to day decision-making. The mechanisms used, and data presented, were extremely diverse with instances of both peers and managers contributing to the assessment process. The criteria for judging effectiveness varied according to the task, the job or role, and the location of the assessor. Perceptions of competence or effectiveness were distributed across a network or community of practice and the extent to which judgements could be made varied with the location of both performer and assessor. Although gender and ethnicity were not directly cited as significant components in this process, work status (grade and length of service) and sometimes location within the organisation were highlighted as affecting the perceived validity of judgements. At times the system was completely opaque with comments or judgements made indirectly. Managerial judgements both by and about the learners were the product of a complex social system in which formal hierarchy played a part but in which other routes could be used. At one level this might be considered organic in the sense that specific processes and mechanisms were developed as part of the development of the social system rather than in any pre-determined way; however, the choice of what information to use needs to be perceived within a context in which performance rather than learning is the prime purpose.

The linkage between the two systems can be seen through the role of the line manager. Work-based assessment relies heavily on the individual line manager both for the collection of data and the process of judgement. This is often specified within the formal process but the line manager also plays a key role in informal processes. Although data can be derived from a range of sources – subordinates, peers and customers - it is the manager who makes judgement decisions and, where appropriate, awards a grade or reward. Within the traditional appraisal process the line manager is explicitly identified as data source, data collector and data evaluator. This is not to say that he or she is the sole source, as the informal system provides the manager with information. Some participants also pointed to a variation of the traditional appraisal based around data provided by the individual employee to support a claim of competence. This latter could be described as a process of negotiation in which the outcome or grade would be determined through presentation and sometimes counter presentation of data. The research also considered the outcomes of assessment in terms of decisions made about the learners and the information provided to them. In the case of the academic system the outcomes are marks or grades and feedback. In the case of formal work assessment the outcomes usually came in the form of a learning or personal development plan, although work targets were also included and some systems had a linkage to payment. The informal system by contrast was seen to influence day to day decisions such as work allocation and was also believed to confer status through perceived competence.

Perhaps the most interesting aspect of this study is not the learners' perceptions of the assessment systems but their reactions and responses to them. Earlier evidence from the academic assessment process suggested that some learners seemed to be avoiding critical analysis and in particular critical comment on the work domain. For example, topics such as organisational change, which are recognised to be problematic for organisations, were sometimes represented as a linear series of planned coherent steps. The focus group discussions revealed a parallel concealment of academic knowledge at work. Some learners were reluctant to demonstrate competence based on academic knowledge in an environment which preferred actual experience and in some cases specific organisational experience. The results point to an interaction between different assessment systems in terms of their influence on student behaviour and the discussions suggest that there is an emergent self managed process involving choice about the presentation of self in different contexts for different purposes. This aspect of self presentation is discussed more extensively below; however, it is important to note that, at least in forms of work-based assessment, learners are making clear purposeful choices about what evidence they present.

What emerges from the research is a complex pattern of activities through which learners seek to manage themselves within the assessment processes. Far from being a simple act of integration or synthesis, learners choose what sorts of evidence they present about their competence and are careful about presenting themselves to different audiences for different purposes. Whilst there is some agreement that the processes of academic and work place assessment may share common elements, the selection of what, where and above all how to present different sorts of evidence is key to understanding how learners interact with assessment. Solomon and Boud (2003) note the reluctance of participants to label themselves 'learners' and point to the negative connotations of this term in relation to lack of status through a related lack of competence. The title of learner is associated with novice or less than effective performer.

To this extent the assessment process can be considered to either affirm or disaffirm claims of competence with different claims being made in different assessment contexts. Holmes (2005) suggests that the claim for competence at work is assisted by the possession of a formal qualification and that therefore such claims could be legitimized through the educational assessment process. Data from this study suggests that claims for competence at work could either be seen as completely separate from academic qualification or related. However, rather than simply reinforce work place views, there is a risk that academic knowledge or status - which might be used to further a claim - could be used by the organisation to disaffirm competence. In other words, learners, in representing academic knowledge in a domain which fails to recognise it or recognises it as of limited value, could become open to a disaffirmation of the identity of the worker as competent practitioner.

This process of managing professional identity is crucial to the learner and the recognition that academic and work-based systems are separate and not fully aligned is important to the way in which claims can be made and affirmed. Evidence of achievement in one context is not directly transferable to another and what may be perceived by academia in terms of critical thinking could be interpreted within the work place as arrogance or even disaffection. These distinctions are important to the process of managing learning and identity at both an individual and institutional level. Beaney (2004) suggests that there is a need on the part of the provider to promote some form of distancing from the practitioner role in order to create reflective space. This research suggests that this space is partially expressed in the distance between the two assessment processes and that, to some extent, the recognition of this space is being used by students themselves in managing their learning. What it also points to is that the results of this navigation by learners are not always fully available to the employer or educational provider through the assessment process. What is actually presented by learners to the different parties may differ considerably according to the perceived purpose and outcomes of the process. Some elements of what is learned within higher education are deliberately not presented directly to the employer and the learner is therefore reliant on these being recognised and validated by the educational provider.

Conclusions

The first and most obvious conclusion is that there are significant differences between academic assessment and work-based assessment. A second conclusion is that the differences between, and sometimes within, work places are sufficient to prevent any single characterisations of a common work-based approach. Thirdly, and perhaps most positively, there is evidence to suggest that learners, rather than being confused or disadvantaged by this possible duality, are actively managing the assessment process as a means of demonstrating their competence or managing their identity in different contexts. According to Biggs (1999) a "good teaching system aligns teaching method and assessment to the learning activities stated in the objectives, so that all aspects of this system are in accord in supporting appropriate learning". Work-based learning represents a challenge to this approach since elements of the method and significant aspects of the assessment process are beyond the control of the learning provider. Rather than seek to control the process academic institutions would do better to try to develop a better understanding of how and why work place assessment operates and use this understanding to create mechanisms to enable learners to manage the process.

The data show that learners are already seeking to manage the assessment process as a mechanism for claiming the status or identity of a competent manager. This requires an understanding of the assessment process but also skills to be able to identify the informal processes operating at work. This in turn suggests a more extensive system of support for individual learning; beyond simple planning to a more active management of the learning process. This notion of learner independence is one of the fundamental concerns of work-based learning but has sometimes proved difficult to operationalise within more formal academic environments. The evidence presented here indicates a need to develop further the notion of an independent learner working towards a personalised set of goals which can be translated into and presented as work place performance. This research confirms the need for students to develop 'navigation' skills as part of meta-cognition or learning to learn. This includes the ability to recognise both formal and informal processes at work. It also involves the ability to manage the dual identities of the learner within higher education and the manager at work, and the dual trajectories that these two changing identities entail.

If we are to assign learners individual responsibility for fitting together the different assessment systems we must provide not only skills but also support and this has implications at an institutional level. Passing responsibility to the learner for managing this engagement does not remove the need for effective liaison with employers. Indeed, it could be argued that to enable this process the relationship needs to be closer and more symbiotic. This means less emphasis on formal 'representative' structures within Foundation degrees and more engagement and activity at a tactical level with local managers. The role of the line manager within the system of work place assessment is crucial and if we are to support students, individual managers also need support. Rather than seek to assimilate the line managers and make them become academic assessors we should seek to understand how work-based assessment operates and provide the line manager with a better understanding of how this process could be improved. This is not to say that formal 'assessment' training is without value but that such attempts to create artificial attributes such as reliability should not overshadow less intrusive approaches to support learning.

Some of the implications for research relate to the limitations of this study. Larger sample sizes are always of benefit but in this context it would also be useful to include cross discipline groups operating within multiple contexts. The range of contexts or settings could also include more and less formalised work-based assessment; it would be particularly useful, for example, to contrast the current sample with learners whose contexts involved more explicit or shared standards of performance or more formalised assessment regimes. A second implication relates to the depth of the research and the need to examine the role and status of the learner within their community, in particular to explore their role in managing the process of changing identity. Greater depth could also include an expanded remit looking at learning within the employment relationship and the employer's perceptions and purposes regarding both their own and academic assessment. Research of this type would examine the significance of context, in terms of both structure and learning culture, and the role of the line manager within the learning process. Finally, it is useful to consider this research within the context of relationships between employers and universities. To some extent this type of research represents boundary crossing by universities into the realm of work, it provides us not only with a better understanding of work-based learning but also with a better understanding of work itself. To fulfil this, educational research needs to take on institutional as well as individual focus but in doing so avoid the simple instrumentalism which sees higher education solely as a means of enhancing skills and production because to be of value research must offer a genuinely critical perspective on learning at work.

References

Armstrong, M. and Baron (1998) *Performance Management – the new realities.* Institute for Professional Development.

Beaney, P. (2004) 'Founded on work? Work-based learning and Foundation degrees' *forward,* Issue 2.

Biggs, J.B. (2003) *Teaching for Quality Learning at University.* Buckingham: Open University Press/SRHE.

Billett, S. (2004) 'Workplace participatory practices - conceptualising workplaces as learning environments', *Journal of Workplace Learning,* v.16, n.6.

Boud, D. (ed.) (1998) *Current Issues and New Agendas in Workplace Learning.* Adelaide: National Centre for Vocational Education Research.

Boud, D. and Solomon, N. (eds.) (2001). *Work-Based Learning: a new higher education?* Buckingham: SRHE and Open University Press.

Burrell, W. G. and Morgan, G. (1979) *Sociological Paradigms and Organisational Analysis.* London: Heinemann.

Brown, S. and Glasner, A. (1999) *Assessment Matters in Higher Education.* SHRE.

Challis, M. (2005) 'The assessment of work based learning – what is the role of employers?', *forward,* Issue 7.

Crooks, T.J. (1988) 'The impact of classroom evaluation practices on students', *Review of Educational Research,* v.58, n.4.

CSHE http://www.cshe.unimelb.edu.au/assessinglearning/05/index.html
Accessed 1 May 2006

Elton, L. and Laurillard, D. (1979) 'Trends in research on student learning', *Studies in Higher Education,* v.4.

fdf (n.d.) *Work based learning – briefing for learning providers*
http://www.fdf.ac.uk/uploads/WorkBasedLearning-breifv2.pdf accessed 1 May 2006

Fletcher, C and Williams R. (1992) *Performance Appraisal and Career Development.* Stanley Thomas

Fuller, A. and Unwin, L. (2003) 'Fostering workplace learning: looking through the lens of apprenticeship', *European Educational Research Journal,* v. 2, n.1.

Gibbs, G. (1999) 'Using assessment strategically to change the way students learn' in Brown, S. and Glasner, A. *Assessment Matters in Higher Education.* SHRE.

Hall, L. Torrington, D. and Taylor, P. (2005) *Human Resource Management.* Essex: Prentice-Hall.

Hendry C, Woodward, S. A., Bradley, P. and Perkins, S. J. (2000) 'Performance and Rewards: cleaning out the stables', *Human Resource Management Journal,* v.10, n.3.

Hennessy, T. and Sawchuk, P. (2003) 'Worker responses to technological change in the Canadian public sector: issues of learning and labour process', *The Journal of Workplace Learning,* v.15, n.7/8.

Holmes, L. (2005) 'Becoming a graduate, becoming a manager: the warranting of emergent identity'. Paper presented at *Critique and Inclusivity: Opening the Agenda,* the 4th International Critical Management Studies Conference July 2005.

Hutchings, P, (ed.) (2002). *The Ethics of Inquiry: issues in the scholarship of teaching and learning.* Menlo Park, CA: The Carnegie Foundation for the Advancement of Teaching.

Huzzard, T. (2004) 'Communities of domination? Reconceptualising organisational learning and power' *The Journal of Workplace Learning,* v.16, n.6.

Lave J & Wenger E, (1991) *Situated Learning: legitimate peripheral participation.* Cambridge: University of Cambridge Press.

Moore, D. (2004) 'An educational perspective on the workplace as a learning environment', *The Journal of Workplace Learning,* v.16, n.6.

Poikela, E. (2004) 'Developing criteria for knowing and learning at work: towards context based assessments', *The Journal of Workplace Learning,* v.16, n.5.

Ramsden, P. (2003) *Learning to Teach in Higher Education.* London: (2nd Ed) Routledge.

Simmonds (2002) 'An expert witness perspective on performance appraisal in universities and colleges', *Employee Relations,* v.24, n.1.

Solomon, N. and Boud, D. (2003) "I don't think I am a learner': acts of naming learners at work', *The Journal of Workplace Learning,* v.15, n.7-8: 326-331.

4

Appendices

Appendix 1

Bibliography of Research and Scholarship Regarding Foundation Degrees

Introduction

It is very difficult to find literature on Foundation degrees which is both well researched and written. It is even more difficult to find material which is specific to particular subjects, sectors or regions. However, the literature is developing and this bibliography is intended to be a contribution to the development of the literature by making what is available known to others.

Notes:

1.   This bibliography refers to published and unpublished works as well as other resources – such as on-line materials – which relate directly and substantially to Foundation degrees. It doesn't include, however, resources which relate indirectly or in part to Foundation degrees in relation, for example, to studies of work-based progression.

2. Some items will be mentioned more than once since the bibliography is arranged in terms of themes and some items will relate to more than one theme. An unpublished research report on Foundation degrees in health, for example, will be included both under 'Health Foundation degrees' and 'Research Reports (unpublished)'.

3. Where articles have been published in professional journals they are only included here if they have a clear basis in research or scholarship. This isn't to make judgements about the value of either literature but rather to keep this bibliography focused on work derived from research and scholarship and to keep it to a manageable length.

4. Unpublished conference papers are not included due to problems of accessibility.

Contents

1. APEL (accreditation of prior experiential learning)
2. Case studies
3. Design and development
4. Early Years Foundation degrees
5. E-learning
6. Employer involvement
7. Engineering Foundation degrees
8. Foundation Degree Forward
9. Foundation degrees: general works
10. Flexible learning
11. Governmental publications
12. HE and Foundation degrees
13. HE in FE
14. Health and Social Care Foundation degrees
15. Information, advice and guidance
16. Market demand
17. Media Foundation degrees
18. Partnerships and progression
19. Policing Foundation degrees
20. Policy issues
21. QAA documents
22. Quality assurance
23. Regional studies
24. Research reports (unpublished)
25. Researching Foundation degrees
26. Teaching and Learning Support Foundation degrees
27. Work-based learning
28. Widening participation

APEL

Challis, M. (2005) 'The Accreditation of Prior Experiential Learning (APEL)', *forward*, Issue 5

Case studies

Barker, R. (2005) 'The Railway Engineering Foundation degree – a case study', *forward*, Issue 4

Harvey, M. et al (2005) 'Work based learning: an Open University case study', *forward*, Issue 5

Lockley, E. (2005) 'Case study – flexible delivery. Health and medical sciences: Paramedic Pathway. St George's Hospital medical School and Kingston University', *forward*, Issue 4

Nicholls, M. et al (2005) 'Validation and quality assurance of Foundation degrees: a case study of a Foundation degree in policing', *forward*, Issue 5

Sutcliffe, J. (2005) 'Developing a flexible delivery method for the Foundation degree in teaching and learning support: a case study of Edge Hill', *forward*, Issue 6

Design and development

Morgan, A. et al (2004) 'Critical reflections on the development of a Foundation Degree', *Research in Post-Compulsory Education,* Vol. 9. No. 3

Early Years Foundation degrees

Phillips, S. (2005) *Barriers to Recruitment to the Foundation Degree in Early Years (Surestart Recognised) and Identification of Staff and Workforce Development Needs in the Gloucestershire Early Years Sector.* Commissioned and Co-Funded by: Gloucestershire Early Years and Childcare Service and the University of Gloucestershire Foundation Degree Office. Unpublished Report

Tait, K., and O'Keefe, J. (2004) 'An examination of the UK Early Years Foundation Degree and the evolution of Senior Practitioners enhancing work-based practice by engaging in reflective and critical thinking', *International Journal of Early Years Education,* Vol. 12. No. 1

E-learning

Marsh, D., and Bennett, S. (2003) 'Widening participation and e-learning: meeting the challenge with a foundation degree', *Widening Participation and Lifelong Learning,* Vol. 5. No. 3

Employer involvement

Challis, M. (2005) 'The assessment of work-based learning: what is the role of employers?' *forward*, Issue 7. Lichfield: *fdf*

Connor, H. (2005) 'Employer engagement', *forward*, Issue 4

Hearsum, A. (2004) 'The business case for Foundation degrees', *forward,* Issue 3

Hearsum, A. (2005) 'Reaching out to employers', *forward*, Issue 4

Engineering Foundation degrees

Barker, R. (2005) 'The Railway Engineering Foundation degree – a case study', *forward*, Issue 4

Foundation Degree Forward

Longhurst, D. (2004) 'Foundation Degree Forward', *Educational Development*, Issue 5.1

Foundation degrees: general works

Blewitt, J. (2005) 'Reconfiguring higher education: the case of foundation degrees', *Education + Training,* Vol. 47, Nos. 2-3

Brennan, L. and Gosling, D. (eds) (2004) *Making Foundation Degrees Work.* Brentwood: SEEC

Yorke, M. (2005) 'Firming the foundations: an empirical and theoretical appraisal of the foundation degree in England', *Widening Participation and Lifelong Learning,* Vol. 7. No. 1

Wilson, J.P. et al (2005) 'Reconfiguring higher education: the case of foundation degrees', *Education + Training,* Vol. 47. No. 2

Flexible learning

Challis, M. (2005) 'Challenging issues for Foundation degree providers... flexible delivery', *forward,* Issue 4

Governmental publications

DfEE (2000) *Foundation Degrees: consultation paper.* February 2000. Nottingham: DfEE

DfES (2003) *Foundation Degrees: meeting the need for higher level skills.* London: DfES

Foundation Degree Support Team (2002) *Foundation Degree National Event. Report on the Second Foundation Degree National Event.* 22 October 2002. University of East London

Foundation Degree Support Team (2002) *Types of Foundation Degree: a case study approach.* A report to HEFCE by the Foundation Degree Support Team. October 2002

Foundation Degree Taskforce (2004) *Foundation Degree Taskforce Report to Ministers.* DfES

HEFCE (2000) *Foundation degree prospectus.* July 2000. Bristol: HEFCE

HEFCE (2001) *Foundation degrees: report on funded projects.* HEFCE 01/40. June 2001. Bristol: HEFCE

York Consulting (2004) *Evaluation of Foundation Degrees. Final report.* September 2004. Unpublished report of research commissioned by the DfES

HE and Foundation degrees

Wilson, J.P. et al (2005) 'Reconfiguring higher education: the case of foundation degrees', *Education + Training,* Vol. 47. No. 2

HE in FE (where this explicitly concerns Foundation degrees)

Dixon, J. et al (2005) 'Accessible higher education: meeting the challenges of HE in FE', *forward,* Issue 6

Marks, A. (2002) '2+2 = 'Access': working towards a higher education and further education overlap to facilitate greater adult participation', *Teaching in Higher Education,* Vol. 7. No. 1

Health and Social Care Foundation degrees

Chaney, G. et al (2005) *Building Common Foundations: full report. Identifying a common core curriculum and accreditation framework for Foundation Degrees in Health and Social Care.* Unpublished report. HERDA-SW and NHSU

Conner, T. and McKnight, J. (2003) 'Workforce transformations: building firm foundations', *Nursing Management – UK,* 10.

Lockley, E. (2005) 'Case study – flexible delivery. Health and medical sciences: Paramedic Pathway. St George's Hospital medical School and Kingston University', *forward,* Issue 4

Priestley, J. (2003) 'The foundation degree: an education framework for rehabilitation assistants?' *International Journal of Therapy and Rehabilitation,* Vol. 10. No. 11

Information, advice and guidance

Jackson, C. and Tunnah, E. (2005) *The Information, Advice and Guidance Needs of Foundation Degree Students – report of an AGCAS survey.* Sheffield: AGCAS

Market demand

Gibbs, P. (2001) 'Is the market ready for foundation degrees?' *Higher Education Review,* Vol. 34. No. 1

Media Foundation degrees

Hanney, R. (2005) 'Enhancing capability through problem based learning: a real world context for media practice education', *forward,* Issue 6

Partnerships and progression

Caller, T. (2005) 'What do local sixth form students think of Foundation degrees and vocational qualifications?' *forward,* Issue 7

Foskett, R. (2005) 'Collaborative partnership in the higher education curriculum: a cross sector study of foundation degree development', *Research in Post-Compulsory Education,* Vol. 10. No. 3

Smith, R. and Betts, M. (2003) 'Partnerships and the consortia approach to United Kingdom Foundation Degrees: a case study of benefits and pitfalls', *Journal of Vocational Education and Training,* Vol. 55. No. 2

Stevenson, J. et al (2005) 'Partnerships for Foundation degrees in rural areas', *forward,* Issue 7

Stoney, C. (2005) 'Improving HE/FE partnerships: how far can streamlining quality assurance take us?' *forward,* Issue 6

Wilson, E. (2005) *Ensuring Progression to Higher Level Skills.* Unpublished research report funded by Aimhigher London South Partnership. London: Carshalton College

Policing Foundation degrees

Nicholls, M. et al (2005) 'Validation and quality assurance of Foundation degrees: a case study of a Foundation degree in policing', *forward,* Issue 5

Policy issues

Doyle, M. (2003) 'Discourses of employability and empowerment: Foundation Degrees and Third Way discursive repertoires', *Discourse,* Vol. 24. No. 3

QAA documents

QAA (2002) *Foundation Degree qualification benchmark (final draft)* November 2002. Gloucester: QAA

QAA (2004) *Foundation Degree qualification benchmark* October 2004. Gloucester: QAA

QAA (2003) *QAA overview report on Foundation Degree reviews (conducted in 2003)* QAA

QAA (2004) *Foundation Degree Qualification Benchmark.* Gloucester: QAA

QAA (2004) *Handbook for the review of foundation degrees in England: 2004-05.* Gloucester: QAA

QAA (2005) *Report of a survey to follow up Foundation Degree reviews carried out in 2002-2003.* Gloucester: QAA

QAA (2005) *Report of a survey of Foundation degrees converted from existing Higher National Diplomas since 2001.* Gloucester: QAA

QAA (2005) *Learning from reviews of Foundation Degrees in England carried out in 2004-05. Sharing good practice.* Gloucester: QAA

Quality assurance

Stoney, C. (2005) 'Improving HE/FE partnerships: how far can streamlining quality assurance take us?' *forward,* Issue 6

Regional studies

Blackie, P. (2005) 'Foundation degrees in the North West England – part 1', *forward,* Issue 6.

Brown, B. (2005) 'Foundation degrees in South West England', *forward,* Issue 5.

Dodgson, R. (2004) *Learner Experience of Foundation Degrees in the North East of England: access, support and progression.* Aimhigher: P4P North East.

O'Doherty, E. (2005) *Mapping Foundation Degrees. Research Report Part 1.* Unpublished research report. Aimhigher Greater Manchester funded project. Manchester: Aimhigher.

Pearson, A. (2005) 'Profile of Foundation degrees in the North East of England', *forward,* Issue 5.

Pickford, C. (2005) 'A guide to the development of Foundation degrees in Yorkshire and Humberside', *forward,* Issue 6.

Seiffert, M. (2005) 'A Profile of Foundation degrees in the East of England', *forward,* Issue 5

Thomas, H. (2005) 'Foundation degrees in the South East of England, *forward,* Issue 6

Research reports (unpublished)

Chaney, G. et al (2005) *Building Common Foundations: full report. Identifying a common core curriculum and accreditation framework for Foundation Degrees in Health and Social Care.* Unpublished report. HERDA-SW and NHSU

Dodgson, R. (2004) *Learner Experience of Foundation Degrees in the North East of England: access, support and progression.* Unpublished research report. Aimhigher: P4P North East

O'Doherty, E. (2005) *Mapping Foundation Degrees. Research report Part 1.* Aimhigher Greater Manchester funded research project. Manchester: Aimhigher.

Phillips, S. (2005) *Barriers to Recruitment to the Foundation Degree in Early Years (Surestart Recognised) and Identification of Staff and Workforce Development Needs in the Gloucestershire Early Years Sector.* Commissioned and Co-Funded by: Gloucestershire Early Years and Childcare Service and the University of Gloucestershire Foundation Degree Office

Wilson, E. (2005) *Ensuring Progression to Higher Level Skills.* London: Carshalton College

York Consulting (2004) *Evaluation of Foundation Degrees.* Final report. September 2004. Report of research commissioned by the DfES

Researching Foundation degrees

Beaney, P.W. (2005) 'Researching Foundation degrees: making a case for the relevance of research', *forward,* Issue 4

Beaney, P.W. (2005) 'Researching Foundation Degrees: turning research into practice', *Educational Development*

Beaney, P.W. (2005) 'Foundation degrees: building a research agenda'. Paper presented at the Annual Conference of the British Educational Research Association (BERA), University of Glamorgan, September 2005

Beaney, P.W. (2005) 'Raising the profile of Foundation degree research: a report on *fdf*'s first national research conference', *forward*, Issue 7

Longhurst, D. (2004) 'Foundation degree forward: research programme'. *forward*, Issue 2

Smith, C. et al (2005) 'A research-led approach to establishing Foundation Degrees', *Research in Post-Compulsory Education*, Vol. 10. No. 1

Teaching and Learning Support Foundation degrees

Edmond, N. (2004) 'The foundation degree as evidence of a new higher education: a study of HE provision for teaching assistants', *Higher Education Review*, Vol. 34. No. 1

Sutcliffe, J. (2005) 'Developing a flexible delivery method for the Foundation degree in Teaching and Learning Support: a case study of Edge Hill', *forward*, Issue 6

Work Based Learning

Beaney, P.W. (2005) 'All in a day's work? Unravelling the conceptual tangles around work-based learning and Foundation degrees', *forward*, Issue 4

Blauciak, M. (2005) 'Work placement, work related, in the work place, simulated work …', *forward*, Issue 3

Challis, M. (2005) The assessment of work-based learning: what is the role of employers?' *forward*, Issue 7

Challis, M. (2005) 'Challenging issues: work-based learning', *forward*, Issue 5.

Harvey, M. et al (2005) 'Work based learning: an Open University case study', *forward*, Issue 5

Taylor, C. (2005) 'The assessment of work-based learning in Foundation degrees', *forward*, Issue 6

Widening participation

Dixon, J. et al (2005) 'Accessible higher education: meeting the challenges of HE in FE', *forward,* Issue 6

Longhurst, D. (2005) 'Are Foundation degrees designed for widening participation? 'Is the Foundation degree a turtle or a fruit fly?', in Duke, C. and Layer, G. (eds) *Widening Participation: which way forward for English higher education?* Leicester: NIACE/Action on Access

Marks, A. (2002) '2+2 = 'Access': working towards a higher education and further education overlap to facilitate greater adult participation', *Teaching in Higher Education,* Vol. 7. No. 1

Marsh, D. and Bennett, S. (2003) 'Widening participation and e-learning: meeting the challenge with a foundation degree', *Widening Participation and Lifelong Learning,* Vol. 5. No. 3

Yorke, M. (2005) 'Firming the foundations: an empirical and theoretical appraisal of the foundation degree in England', *Widening Participation and Lifelong Learning,* Vol. 7. No. 1

Appendix 2

Researching Foundation Degrees: contacts and resources to support research

Foundation degree research is in its infancy. It is important, therefore, to provide some support for researchers, scholars and practitioners who want to engage in Foundation degree research and scholarship in whatever form this might take. This appendix, therefore, provides information regarding key contacts and websites which might be useful in developing research and practice regarding Foundation degrees. The list contains organisations which are engaged in 'practice' as well as research. All of the information is correct at the time of writing but both institutions and web addresses unfortunately come and go!

Action on Access
www.actiononaccess.org

Aimhigher
www.aimhigher.ac.uk

Aimhigher JISCmail
www.jiscmail.ac.uk/lists/aimhigher.html

Aimhigher National Mentoring Scheme
www.hementornet.org

Applied Educational Research Scheme (AERS)
www.aers.org.uk

Apprenticeships
www.apprenticeships.org.uk

Association of Colleges (AoC)
www.aoc.co.uk

Association of Learning Providers (ALP)
www.learningproviders.org.uk

BBC Aimhigher
www.bbc.co.uk/schools/aimhigher

British Educational Research Association (BERA)
www.bera.ac.uk

Careers Research and Advisory Centre (CRAC)
www.crac.org.uk

Centre for Education and Industry (University of Warwick)
www.warwick.ac.uk/cei/

Centre for Higher Education Research and Information (CHERI)
www.open.ac.uk/cheri/index.htm

Connexions
www.connexions.gov.uk

Department for Education and Skills (DfES)
www.dfes.gov.uk

DfES foundationdegree.org.uk
www.foundationdegree.org.uk/

DfES Research
http://www.dfes.gov.uk/research/

Economic and Social Research Council (ESRC)
www.esrc.ac.uk

Edexcel
http://www.edexcel.org.uk/home/

European Access Network (EAN)
www.ean-edu.org

Evidence for Policy and Practice Information (EPPI) Centre
http://eppi.ioe.ac.uk/EPPIWeb/home.aspx

FD Research JISCmail
http://www.jiscmail.ac.uk/lists/FD-RESEARCH.html

Forum for Access and Continuing Education (FACE)
http://www.f-a-c-e.org.uk/

Foundation Degree Forum JISCmail
http://www.jiscmail.ac.uk/lists/FOUNDATION-DEGREE-FORUM.html

Foundation Degree Forward (*fdf*)
www.fdf.ac.uk

Further Education News
http://www.FEnews.co.uk

HE Academy
http://www.heacademy.ac.uk/

HE Academy Subject Network
http://www.heacademy.ac.uk/SubjectNetwork.htm

Higher Education Careers Services Unit (HECSU)
http://www.hecsu.ac.uk/cms/ShowPage/Home_page/p!eeXLbLc

Higher Education and Research Opportunities in the UK (HERO)
http://www.hero.ac.uk/uk/home/index.cfm

Higher Education Funding Council for England (HEFCE)
www.hefce.ac.uk/learning/founddeg/

Higher Education Statistics Agency (HESA)
http://www.hesa.ac.uk/

Institute of Education (University of London)
http://ioewebserver.ioe.ac.uk/ioe/index.html

Joint Information Systems Committee (JISC)
http://www.jisc.ac.uk/

JISCmail
http://www.jiscmail.ac.uk/index.htm

Learning and Skills Council (LSC)
http://www.lsc.gov.uk/National/default.htm

Learning and Skills Research Centre (LSRC)
www.LSRC.ac.uk

Learning and Skills Development Agency (LSDA)
http://www.lsda.org.uk
(NB. The LSDA has recently, in 2006, become two new agencies: the LSN and QIA)

Learning and Skills Network (LSN)
http://www.lsneducation.org.uk/

National Centre for Research Methods (NCRM)
www.ncrm.ac.uk

National Educational Research Forum (NERF)
www.nerf-uk.org/

National Institute of Adult Continuing Education (NIACE)
http://www.niace.org.uk/

Office for Fair Access (OFFA)
www.offa.org.uk

Prospects UK
http://www.prospects.ac.uk/cms/ShowPage/Home_page/p!eLaXi

Qualifications and Curriculum Authority (QCA)
www.qca.org.uk

Quality Assurance Agency for Higher Education (QAA)
http://www.qaa.ac.uk/

Quality Improvement Agency (QIA)
http://www.qia.org.uk/

Regard on-line database
http://www.regard.ac.uk/

Research Assessment Exercise (RAE)
www.rae.ac.uk

Research Capacity Building Network (ESRC/TLRP)
www.cardiff.ac.uk/socsi/capacity

Research Informed Practice Site
www.standards.dfes.gov.uk/research/

Sector Skills Development Agency (SSDA)
www.ssda.org.uk

Society for Research into Higher Education (SRHE)
www.srhe.ac.uk

Student finance
www.direct.gov.uk/studentfinance

Teaching and Learning Research Programme (TLRP)
www.tlrp.org

Times Educational Supplement (TES)
http://www.tes.co.uk

Times Higher Educational Supplement (THES)
http://www8.thes.co.uk/

Training and Development Agency for Schools (TDA)
http://www.tda.gov.uk/

Transforming Learning Cultures in FE
http://www.ex.ac.uk/sell/tlc/homepage.htm

Universities UK
www.universitiesuk.ac.uk

Universities Vocational Awards Council (UVAC)
http://www.uvac.ac.uk/